From Bobby to Babylon
Blacks and the British Police

b

From Bobby to Babylon
Blacks and the British Police

Darcus Howe

From Bobby to Babylon: Blacks and the British Police
by Darcus Howe

First published by Race Today Publications, April 1988
165 Railton Road, London SE24 OLU

This edition published by Bookmarks in 2020

© Bookmarks Publications Ltd
c/o 1 Bloomsbury Street, London WC1B 3QE
www.bookmarksbookshop.co.uk

ISBN 978-1-912926-39-8 paperback
ISBN 978-1-912926-40-4 Kindle
ISBN 978-1-912926-41-1 epub
ISBN 978-1-912926-42-8 pdf

Typeset by Bookmarks Publications
Cover design by Ben Windsor
Printed by Halstan & Co

*For Hass, Bertie, Ambrosia, Dibbie,
Johnny Qui, Mikey, Marvs, Matts, Staffo,
Tom Strokes and Stafford Scott*

Publishers' Note

This selection of articles by Darcus Howe were all previously published elsewhere, but were collected here together for the original 1988 edition of this book.

The first three articles were published in the journal *Race Today* under the heading 'From Bobby to Babylon: Blacks and the British Police'. (Vol 12, no 1, May/June 1980; Vol 12, no 2, November 1980 and Vol 14, no 2, February/March 1982). Darcus Howe was editor of Race Today 1974–1985.

'Scarman: Failing to Grasp the Nettle' was first published under the title 'My Fears after this Failure' in *The Times* 26 November, 1981, as an invited response to the *Scarman Report, The Brixton Disorders*, 10–12 April, 1981.

The interview with Darcus Howe was taken from *Revolt of the Underclass* by Alexander Cockburn and James Ridgeway and was first published in the *Village Voice*, 6–12 January, 1982. 'The Shoe that didn't Pinch' was published in *The Guardian* 28 January, 1982.

'Is a Police Carnival' and 'Race Today and the Struggle for Racial Justice' are new to this edition of the book and are reproduced with the kind permission of the editors of *Here to Stay, Here to Fight: A Race Today Anthology*, edited by Paul Field, Robin Bunce, Leila Hassan, Margaret Peacock, published by Pluto Press, London in 2020.

A Note on Terminology

Both in the title and throughout this book, Darcus Howe uses the term "Black" or occasionally "Black and multiracial." We acknowledge and respect the fact that in recent decades there has been a shift away from the use of these terms and a preference for wider terms such as Black and Asian, Black, Asian and Minority Ethnic, or even BAME. Black was the language of the time in which the articles were written and we feel it is right that as a historical document, the book should stand in its original form.

Two points should be added however. Firstly, the terms "black" and "blackness" were adopted and recognised as collective terms which encouraged solidarity among groups of different ethnic origin by focusing on the common experience of racism rather than dwelling on the areas of difference. As we have observed elsewhere, Darcus was an internationalist who would have been acutely aware that very few people benefitted from the obsession with distinct and separate identities that developed in the aftermath of the great struggles of the 1960s and 70s.

People should have the right to define themselves in whatever way they feel most comfortable. The aim of this book is not to marginalise and exclude but rather, to encourage unity.

Contents

Foreword

In spite of the victories won in the struggles of black people against police and judicial injustice, in spite of the revelation of institutionalised racism in the police force, the protracted war of attrition against young black people continues. Racial profiling is common practice; the astonishing rise in the incidence of black deaths at the hands of the police during the 1980s and 90s continues; and the culture of impunity has become even more entrenched.

Darcus Howe's *From Bobby To Babylon* is an important historical document. This collection of engaging articles on the black experience of British policing during the turbulent 1970s and 80s exhibit Howe's journalism at its finest: analytical, empirical, combative and lucid, always mindful of historical context.

Linton Kwesi Johnson
November 2019

Introduction to the 2020 edition

"Darcus Howe is a West Indian"

This is how CLR James, the great Trinidadian Marxist characterised his nephew Rhett Radford Leighton Howe. Darcus himself would later modify this, introducing himself as "a West Indian and he lives in Britain".

As Robin Bunce and Paul Field highlight in their brilliant biography *Renegade — The Life and Times of Darcus Howe*, there is so much meaning in those two simple sentences. West Indians have a very specific history rooted in slavery and colonialism. Both James and Howe were keen students of that history and dedicated their lives to exploding the myth that black people have always been simply the passive victims of our predicament. Instead they sought to illuminate and encourage the continuation of a rich tradition of struggle against slavery, racism and exploitation.

Howe was born in Trinidad in 1943 and grew up in an island which like many British colonies was in the throes of shaking off imperial rule. For over 50 years, though, after docking at Southampton in 1961 he played a critical role in the struggle against racism in his adopted homeland.

One of the places that Darcus worked at in those early years was the El Rio, a cafe in Notting Hill — which was owned by his friend and fellow Trinidadian Frank Crichlow. In 1968, Critchlow established the Mangrove restaurant in All Saints Road also in Notting Hill.

El Rio and Mangrove were places where black and white people met and mixed easily. The BBC had recently relocated to nearby White City, so both were places where middle class whites, socialites and one or two notorious politicians were happy to eat and enjoy the vibe. Not surprisingly this did not meet with the approval of the police and neither did the presence of so–called "hustlers", the young unemployed.

The police always treated Mangrove with hostility and

suspicion, constantly looking for reasons to shut it down and prosecute its owners and the activists who frequented it. The premises were raided twelve times between January 1969 and July 1970. The rationale for this was that it was being used as a drugs den, this despite the fact that no evidence of such activity was ever found. Undeterred, the police pursued Crichlow for a series of petty licensing irregularities such as allowing dancing and providing food and tea after 11pm.

Darcus had also worked at Mangrove but was back in Trinidad for a period of time, participating in a Black Power Rebellion on the island of his birth when the harassment began. On his return to London, Crichlow told him about this turn of events. At that time Darcus was a member of the British Black Panthers and, inspired by the ideas of their American counterparts, he suggested a demonstration.

The demonstration took place on 9 August 1970. It was a modest affair with perhaps 150 vociferous participants. They were confronted by 700 police who waded into the crowd and arrested 19 people. Nine of them, Crichlow, Howe, Barbara Beese, Rupert Boyce, Rhodan Gordon, Anthony Innis, Althea Lecointe, Rothwell Kentish and Godfrey Millett were subsequently prosecuted for various offences including conspiring to incite a riot, affray and assaulting police officers.

The subsequent trial demonstrated two of Howe's great attributes. Emboldened by his education at Trinidad's prestigious Queen's Royal College and a grounding in the law from a period of study at Middle Temple, he could certainly talk the talk. Instead of relying upon barristers to represent them, he and Althea Lecointe Jones conducted their own defence. They worked in collaboration with the other defendants' lawyers who included Ian Macdonald, one of the finest radical barristers of the era, who sadly passed away as this republication was being produced.

What the trial also demonstrated therefore was that Howe could "walk the walk". He passionately believed in oppressed and exploited people doing things for themselves, rather than relying upon others to lead their struggles.

As Darcus documents here in *Cause for Concern — In the Public Eye*, one of the defendants' tactics was to demand an all-black jury on the grounds that only such a panel represented the peers by whom they should be tried. Their tenacity is highlighted by the fact that they argued the case for two days. The court ruled against them, but they succeeded in putting the prosecution on the defensive and highlighting the political nature of the police conduct. Eventually they were able to dismiss some 63 prospective jurors and ensure that there were two black people on the jury.

The trial took place at the Old Bailey in late 1971 and lasted for 55 days with the police evidence centering around accusations that Mangrove was "a haunt for criminals, prostitutes and ponces". It was a desperate case and at the end of it all nine were acquitted of riot. Five of them, including crucially both Crichlow and Howe were acquitted of all other charges.

The lessons learned during struggles such as this and his activism in the Black Power Rebellion in 1970 in Trinidad informed Howe's editorship of the magazine *Race Today* between 1973 and 1988 and his outstanding broadcast work on programmes such as *Black on Black*, *The Bandung File* and *Devil's Advocate*. The articles that are included in this collection were written during that time and published under the title *From Bobby To Babylon — Blacks and the British Police*.

The title encapsulates a dramatic change in perceptions and understanding about the role and behaviour of the constabulary. From the 1950s onwards, the popular image of the police was that of the kindly Constable George Dixon characterised in the long running BBC television series *Dixon of Dock Green*. Police officers were affectionately known as "Bobbies", a reference to their founder the 19th century Home Secretary and later Prime Minister Sir Robert Peel. By the time Howe came to write these articles, the harsh realities that he documented had led Britain's black communities to classify them in more sinister terms. "Babylon" was a word widely used by the increasingly influential and growing population of Rastafarians and adopted by black youth to classify their oppressors.

Darcus was not simply commentating on these matters but also speaking from personal experience. Mangrove would not prove to be the only time he would feel the long arm of the law. He was arrested six times whilst he was editor of *Race Today* and on five occasions he was acquitted of all charges. When he was sent to prison for three months for assault in 1977, a national and international campaign led to his release in a week.

From Bobby to Babylon is reproduced here in full for a number of reasons. It has been out of print for many years and, consequently, too few people particularly from younger generations know about it. Until now, those wishing to read it would need to know someone who had a copy or have access to one of the handful of libraries that retain one. It is certainly worth reading both as a chronicle of its time and an intervention in a series of tumultuous struggles, notably the urban uprisings that occurred in 1981 and the struggle for justice for 13 young black people killed in a likely racist arson attack in the New Cross Fire in South London.

Howe was one of the main organisers of the magnificent 20,000 strong Black People's Day of Action that was called in the aftermath of that blaze. At the heart of the campaign was anger at the dismissive and complacent response of the police, politicians and media. "Thirteen dead, nothing said" was the rallying cry of the protesters and the culmination of years of police harassment and brutality. The Brixton uprising followed a month later.

Though the articles here were all written between 1980 and 1982, the collection was first published in 1988. Without doubt they were still of relevance to the struggles that had subsequently ensued in a decade dominated by the divisive premiership of Margaret Thatcher. Notable among these were the riots that once again erupted in 1985.

Much has happened in the decades since then. One of the most significant was the publication of the Stephen Lawrence Inquiry Report in 1999. That report, written by retired judge Sir William Macpherson was primarily focused on the appalling investigation into the racist murder of 18-year-old student Stephen Lawrence, but also addressed the wider relationship between the police and Britain's black communities. Macpherson reached the landmark conclusion that the investigation, the police more generally, and indeed public bodies across society as a whole are blighted by institutional racism, which he characterised as:

> ...the collective failure of an organisation to provide an appropriate and professional service to people because of their colour, culture or ethnic origin.

It is seen in:

> ...processes, attitudes and behaviour which amount to discrimination through unwitting prejudice, ignorance, thoughtlessness and racist stereotyping which disadvantages minority ethnic people.

There is much that is wrong with this definition but it was nonetheless a huge step forward from another judge, Lord Leslie Scarman's report into the 1981 Brixton riots. Darcus dissects and destroys that earlier report here in *Scarman — Failing to Grasp the Nettle.*

When the Stephen Lawrence Inquiry Report was presented to Parliament, the minister who had commissioned it, Labour Home Secretary Jack Straw promised that it would herald a "step change" in society's attitude to race relations. He accepted all of Macpherson's recommendations, sponsored the Race Relations (Amendment) Act 2000 and set up an advisory group which included Stephen's parents Doreen and Neville Lawrence to monitor progress.

A generation later, politicians, public institutions and the press are adamant in their assertion that the term institutional racism is outdated. Hence in an interview which marked the twentieth anniversary of the report, Metropolitan Police Commissioner Cressida Dick declared: "I don't feel it is now a useful way to describe the Service and I don't believe we are (institutionally racist). I simply don't see it as a helpful or accurate description." This is despite the fact that she acknowledges that at current rates of progress, it would take another 100 years to achieve the level of "ethnic minority" representation within the Metropolitan Police that the report demanded.

More importantly, the factors that had informed the Stephen Lawrence Inquiry remain deeply entrenched. In Macpherson's own words, disproportionality in stops and search had been the single biggest bone of contention expressed by black communities during the inquiry. When he reached that conclusion, black people were four times more likely to be stopped and searched than their white counterparts. In 2019, those identifying as "Black or Black British" are 9.7 times more likely to be stopped than white people.

Meanwhile in 2017 Labour MP David Lammy completed a review of "the treatment of Black, Asian and Minority Ethnic individuals in the Criminal Justice System" that was commissioned by David Cameron's Conservative government. It included a series of damning statistics about arrest rates, Crown Prosecution Service charging decisions, what happens at court — including the advice given to those accused of crimes, the treatment of those imprisoned and rehabilitation in the community. Lammy's depressingly predictable conclusion was that "BAME individuals still face bias including overt discrimination in parts of the justice system". Elsewhere over 1700 people have died following contact with the police since 1990. Another government report written by Dame Elish Angiolini QC examined this and noted with alarm the "disproportionately high number of deaths of black men in restraint related incidents".

None of these inquiries and reports were commissioned out of thin air. Rather, they are the result of struggle. They came about precisely because of the organised and vocal determination of families, campaigners and activists.

It is this tradition that informed Darcus Howe's approach. He was firm in his belief that black people should lead anti-racist campaigns. As students of Howe's writing whether here in this publication, in Bunce and Field's book and in the Race Today Collective's excellent new anthology *Here To Stay, Here To Fight* will note, he could at times be fiercely critical of others who he believed were seeking to infiltrate and control campaigns, including the socialist left. What matters most though is that throughout his life Darcus understood the need for black and white unity in struggle. Indeed, in an interview published here under the title *Revolt of the Underclass*, he is adamant about the importance of class and about the need to build a "black/white mass organisation".

Typically, Darcus didn't just talk a good game. He himself played a leading role in the famous "Battle of Lewisham" in August 1977 that laid the foundations for the establishment of the Anti Nazi League (ANL). In his book *Some Lives! A GP's East End,* David Widgery, a charismatic and radical doctor, Socialist Workers Party member and leading figure in the ANL and its cultural equivalent Rock Against Racism (RAR), painted an unforgettable image of Darcus, "up a lamp post in New Cross, manoeuvring crowds of (anti-fascist) demonstrators to block the National Front's unwelcome passage as if he was setting a Lord's outfield".

Widgery died at the tragically young age of 45 in October 1992 and Darcus was one of the speakers at a commemorative event to mark his passing that December. Paul Foot, another great socialist and campaigning journalist recalled that Darcus ended his contribution with a comment about the experiences of the five children he had fathered in Britain:

> The first four had grown up angry, fighting forever against racism all around them. The fifth child had grown up 'black and at ease'. This 'space' he attributed partly to the work of the ANL and RAR.

Over 40 years on from those momentous events in South East

London it is clear that racism remains deeply entrenched not just in Britain but across the globe. Indeed it is arguable that worldwide the situation is worse than at any time since the 1930s. Despite the failing health of his final years, Darcus remained committed to the fight right up until his death in April 2017.

A notable example of this occurred in 2011 when England experienced another wave of riots in the wake of Mark Duggan's death at the hands of the police in Tottenham. There was a furious reaction from the media and public figures including the then London Mayor Boris Johnson. Meanwhile the courts responded by imposing "exemplary sentences" upon those convicted of offences.

Darcus refused to join the chorus of condemnation. Instead he argued passionately that the eruption had its origins in the continued discrimination and exclusion that blights the lives of black and white working class youth. His exchange with the hapless BBC presenter Fiona Armstrong on the 9th August 2011 went on to become a YouTube sensation.

Included alongside the main text of *From Bobby To Babylon* are two pieces, Darcus's own *Is a Police Carnival?* and Gareth Peirce's *Race Today and The Struggle for Racial Justice* that are also printed in *Here To Stay, Here To Fight.* These two publications and others that will hopefully follow are the result of the Race Today Collective's commitment to share the knowledge and experience that its members accrued over 15 years.

The Collective was born out of a determination to record and recognise the struggles that were taking place against racism in the community, and to be a vehicle for the mobilisation of the community. Following his appointment as *Race Today* editor it was an audacious move by Howe to wrest control away from the then liberal Institute of Race Relations and relocate the publication from Kings Cross in central London to Brixton, Britain's unofficial black capital. From there, and heavily influenced by CLR James, he recruited a team of people including Leila Hassan, Farrukh Dhondy, and Linton Kwesi Johnson who were intent on pursuing a far more radical agenda.

The decision to republish *Here To Stay, Here to Fight* and *From Bobby to Babylon* could not be more timely. At the time of writing Britain is in the midst of a general election campaign during which there is a fierce debate about crime and punishment. More broadly there have been widespread calls across the mainstream media and political spectrum for an increase in police numbers and powers in the face of a significant rise in violent crime. At the same time we are witnessing the unprecedented prosecution of police officers for their role in the 1989 Hillsborough stadium disaster and the death of former footballer Dalian Atkinson in 2016. Both of these have come about as a result of the courage and commitment of those who lost their loved ones.

We began by noting that Darcus was an activist based in Britain and we have noted that *From Bobby to Babylon* was an intervention in the struggle here. The Race Today Collective was always internationalist in its outlook however and this reflected itself in the way in which they supported and participated in the numerous campaigns that they promoted.

It should be clear that the lessons we can learn from these republished works are still of relevance beyond these shores. In particular the emergence of the Black Lives Matter movement during the presidency of Barack Obama has shone a harsh spotlight upon the activities of the police in the United States. Darcus's writings can usefully be read alongside works by the likes of Angela Davis, Alex Vitali, DeRay McKesson, Keeanga–Yamahtta Taylor, Robert Reiner, Michelle Alexander, James Forman Jr, and Bryan Stevenson. They represent a radical critique of the criminal justice system. We hope that contributions such as these and filmmaker Ava DuVernay's outstanding *13th* and *When They See Us* play a role in educating and inspiring a new generation in Britain and elsewhere to stand up for their rights.

Brian Richardson

November 2019

Preface to the 1988 edition

These articles were written out of political necessity. That is to say they are neither academic responses to social phenomena, nor were they generated as a form of self–expression.

In early 1980, the *Race Today* Collective held its annual conference. There, the view emerged that Britain was due for a massive social upheaval of young blacks against the police. This was not vulgar speculation. The membership spent a weekend analysing the historical development of the black struggle against police oppression in Britain, and came to the conclusion that a mass revolt of young blacks was imminent.

As a result I was required by the organisation to write a series of articles in its journal, *Race Today*, which would prepare the readership for the impending revolt. The revolt came in April 1981 after the second article was published. The third article, therefore, was written after the revolt, and completed the task set by the Collective.

On the afternoon of 10 April, 1981, the black youth in Brixton exploded. The entire membership of *Race Today*, with the exception of Linton Kwesi Johnson, who was abroad, met throughout the weekend at its headquarters in Shakespeare Road, Brixton. The offices were located in the seat of the insurrection. The organisation monitored minute by minute what was taking place. At the end of the weekend, 10 April–13 April, *Race Today* members assembled the leaders of the uprising and debriefed them in extensive detail on their activities. The information was taped and transcribed, and after the contents were digested, both the tapes and the transcripts were destroyed.

The government summoned Lord Scarman, one of the nation's Law Lords, to investigate the causes of the revolt which had, by the end of July, spread throughout the black communities in England. He published his report in November 1981. On the day of publication, the editor of *The Times* newspaper telephoned me at the offices of *Race Today* and commissioned a 1,500 word feature article on my responses to the Scarman report. I duly obliged. The perspective of that article was informed, in part, by the material acquired from the leaders of the Brixton revolt. The article which appeared in the *The Times* 26 November, 1981, under the heading *My Fears after this Failure* is reprinted here.

Modern means of communication ensured that news of the uprising spread throughout the world. In November 1981, two journalists from the *Village Voice,* in New York, interviewed me at length at the offices of *Race Today,* on the nature of the revolt and my thoughts on its implications. The result is the fifth article from Revolt of the Underclass by Alexander Cockburn and James Ridgeway. Obviously, there is some repetition. The thoughts and ideas which appeared in the first four articles are further clarified and developed in the interview.

The final article first appeared in *The Guardian* on 28 January, 1982. It recounts a personal encounter with two officers of the Metropolitan Police who arrested me on suspicion of stealing from women's handbags in Central London. I was released within the hour without being charged. I sent a copy of the article to the Commissioner of Police who set in motion the much–touted complaints procedure. Two officers were detailed to investigate and they took statements from Michael Cadette and me. Months later I received a letter stating that there was no basis for taking action against the officers involved.

In the last couple of years, a new generation of young, black activists has emerged. If these articles serve to educate them that their struggles are based in a solid historical foundation then I consider the hours and days spent writing them to be of some use.

Darcus Howe

London, January 1988

Darcus Howe addresses a rally for the Mangrove Nine in Notting Hill, 1971.
Photo: Horace Ove

The Early Years:
Whisper in the Ear of Authority

Perhaps the institution most paraded by British rulers as exemplifying the best in their democratic traditions has been the police force. 'The best of its kind in the world', 'the finest police force of all time', 'an exemplary institution', are but a few examples of the sentiments with which this institution has been regaled. And towering above all police forces in the history of our modem age, they tell us, is that quintessence of order and pioneer of justice, impartiality and good sense, the British bobby.

It appears as though this rare breed of Caucasian men and women is possessed of some unique genetic trait, not to be found in their counterparts in other theatres of the world.

Even the most vulgar propaganda conceals some truth, and only with a dispassionate, historical inspection can the truth about the British police be extricated from the fulsome praises of those whose sole concern is the preservation of a repressive social order.

Summed up briefly, the truth about the British police reads as follows: the mass of the British people, in the process of overthrowing a tyrannical monarchy, has grown alert to the spectre of tyranny. Faced with the greed of the rising bourgeoisie, they have managed, through the centuries, to fight off, successfully, all attempts by a class of would-be tyrants to reassert the brutalities of the preceding age. Though the power swung this way now and that way then, the British public has managed to evolve a modem state which contains some of the checks and balances against outright, totalitarian dictatorship.

In this remarkable balance struck between two classes, the police and armed forces have always remained subordinate to the civil power, hemmed in, as it were, by sets of rules and disciplines. In short, organisational structures tend to reflect that the police are servants of the public and answerable to us.

Time and again, the British police, straining at the leash with which they have been held by the public, have sought to break away, shielded, egged on and encouraged by sections of the bourgeoisie. Firmly they have been returned to what that fine historian, E P Thompson, describes as, "something like a proper place".

The British bobby, therefore, has not been a creature endowed with fine genetic traits, but more a consequence of the partially successful struggles of a people and at times of a class, the working class, to put a firm grip on the tyrannical excesses to which all modern police forces are subject. The British working class has always been central to this process. The modern police force was indeed created for the specific purpose of preventing dock workers from augmenting their wages by appropriating a portion of the goods they were employed to load, unload and distribute. Some 50,000 men and women, a powerful section of the growing army of labour, were concentrated in the port of London there to handle the main commodity, sugar, the product of slave labour in the Caribbean.

The first modern police force was set up in Wapping in 1798 and financed largely by the West India merchants. The sons of merchants were not the ones employed to police the blood-stained wealth of their parents. They, the merchants, would draw the personnel from within the working class itself.

This remains the principle of modern policing, and the working class from that moment has struggled to curb the principal source of its oppression — the police.

Such a struggle found itself on the agenda in the political life of the nation in the mid 1950s. We need catalogue only a few examples which illustrate the rot that set in within the police force at the time.

In 1956, disciplinary action was taken against the then Chief Constable of Cardiganshire following complaints that his force was not properly administered.

In 1957, criminal proceedings were undertaken against the Chief Constable of Brighton and other senior officers. The Chief Constable was acquitted but subsequently dismissed from the force. Two senior police officers were found guilty of corruption and sentenced to imprisonment. Shortly after, the Chief Constable of Worcester was convicted of fraud and sentenced to imprisonment.

At the end of 1957, allegations were made that a young man from Thurso in Scotland was assaulted by two police officers and no effective action had been taken to investigate the truth of the complaint. A parliamentary tribunal found one of the officers guilty of an unjustifiable assault.

In July 1959, Nottingham Watch Committee suspended the Chief Constable who refused to submit a report of police enquiries which concerned a member of the city council. The Home Secretary intervened to reinstate the Chief Constable.

In November 1959, it was raised in Parliament that the Home Secretary made £300 of public money available to settle an action brought against a Constable of the Metropolitan police on grounds of alleged assault.

And so, there was irrefutable evidence before the nation that sections of its police force, ranging from Chief Constable to the most lowly placed officer, were involved a frolic of violence and corruption all their own. The British people, on the other hand, had emerged from the Second World with the sharpest of experiences of just what were the consequences of a police force gone berserk. With unbridled power invested in them, the corrupt German police had left, strewn across continent, the bodies of thousands of European citizens In this post Second World War atmosphere, the British working class displayed a sense of self, a confidence in its own power which drew a grudging respect from its ruling classes. These forces combined to demand of their rulers that a severe check be placed on the developments in the police force.

They succeeded in forcing the Conservative government of the day to set up a Royal Commission on the police. Part of the brief of the Commission was an investigation into the relationship between police and members of the public and the means of ensuring that complaints by the public against the police were effectively dealt with.

Grievances which simmered beneath the surface were brought out into the open. A deluge of complaints poured into the Commission. Evidence given to Commission raised the lid on police corruption. The Conservative Party Bow Group referred to offences of perjury committed by police officers to secure convictions against prisoners; the Law Society emphasised the tendency among police officers to colour and exaggerate evidence; the National Council for Civil Liberties drew attention to police violence, the irregular means of obtaining evidence, the ineptitude in handling processions and in dealing with political and industrial demonstrations.

The Police Federation and Superintendents' Association admitted that relations between police and public had grown worse. The Sottish Police Federation, the Magistrates' Association of England and Wales and members of the legal profession registered that relations were in grave decline.

And the members of the Commission were forced to conclude that there was an overwhelming body of evidence which pointed to police malpractice.

Even so, nothing involving blacks was recorded in those cases which forced the government to set up the Commission. More than that, there was not one statement from those entrusted with the tasks of the enquiry which drew attention to what the police were up to in the black communities.

The only hint to emerge from within official society, that police malpractice was not reserved for whites only, came from the Member of Parliament for Salford West. In the parliamentary debate, which addressed itself to the terms of reference of the Royal Commission, he asked the then Home Secretary whether "the terms of reference would cover the relationship between the police and particularly coloured immigrants".

This blanket silence on the particular experiences of blacks at the hands of the British police, at a moment when the issue was being openly debated, could only serve to reinforce in police officers that their malpractices in the domestic colonies had the sanction of official society and the public at large. In short, the findings of the Commission would strengthen the leash with which the white population held the police at bay, but freedom to go 'nigger hunting' was assured.

And now, it has to be said, that for 25 long years, right here on native soil, the British police have broken free from that leash, and like a horse deranged, trampled wildly through the black communities. In these domestic colonies, no rules apply, disciplines are broken willy-nilly. The British bobby has given way to the boot boy, to the teddy boy in blue. From Bobby to Babylon.

The West Indian Standing Conference, an umbrella body which co-ordinated the activities of a diverse number of small West Indian societies in the UK, wisely recorded for posterity the oppression of the period. The author of *Nigger Hunting in England?* (1966), commissioned by Standing Conference, begins with the boldest of statements:

> For the seven years that I have been residing in Brixton, I have been constantly besieged by members of the immigrant population with matters of conflict between them and members of the Police Force.

The whole tenor of the report indicates that the author

chose his words with a degree of caution. Not 'approached' by members of the immigrant population; not 'lobbied' by members of the immigrant population, but 'besieged'. And besiege him the blacks did.

Somehow, the West Indian's home was not his castle as was the Englishman's. Nor did it seem that the proverbial right of a citizen of the UK to be secure in his dwelling house applied to blacks. Simulate, if you will, the atmosphere at the Brixton or Notting Hill police station on any weekend during the mid fifties.

The police patrol is on the alert for the Blue Beat: should the sound of Prince Buster perhaps drift his way, then all powers of detection were set in motion. A posse of officers would be mobilised to apprehend these criminal subversives who were undermining the fabric of British society.

It was presumed that these perpetrators of the Blue Beat were perforce the vendors of both alcohol and ganja. And in charged the British bobby. In these matters, the general tendency usually surfaces to the outsider in the form of celebrated cases. In 1962, at a house in Mostyn Road, Brixton, a West Indian family invited guests to a party at their home. On information received, police officers at the Brixton police station were led to believe that alcohol was being sold on the premises without a licence. In the name of the law the police violated the threshold of a black home, seized the drinks and charged the head of the household accordingly. The defendants were able to convince the magistrate that a quiet family celebration was simply desecrated by the pioneer of justice, impartiality and good sense, the British bobby.

Then, too, we had that cause célèbre, the 'Wedding Cake' case. Again, Prince Buster activated the forces of law and order. They invaded the home and to the surprise of the West Indians present also seized several gaily wrapped parcels. It took several court hearings of prosecution and defence evidence for the magistrate to realise that the gaily wrapped parcels, the three-tiered iced cake, did not 'fall off the back of a lorry', and that the drinks were in fact freely available for celebrating the union of man and wife.

There is ample evidence that these attacks were orchestrated from above. Sensing the growing criticisms developing within the black community, the police, a force unto itself, had prepared politicians and public alike for the crusade they were conducting in the domestic colonies.

By 1957, a newspaper headline screamed, 'Black Men, Brothel Keeping and Dope', and called for "a tighter supervision on the rash of clubs emerging in the West Indian community". In February of that same year, following a raid on a house where black men were found to be playing cards, the Chief Inspector gave the following interview to the press:

> When the police find a house of this description every endeavour must be made to suppress it. The majority of men are not working. Many have never worked while they have lived in this country and have money from various means.

This view of the black population as engaging in weekend Bacchanalian orgies where alcohol, sex and dope prevailed was well nurtured by the police. It served effectively to cut off and undermine the possibility of opposition from sections of the white population who would otherwise offer support to the black community. But the politicians had given their stamp of approval and expressed their confidence that the police were rightly engaged in stamping out perfidious tendencies which were emerging in the black community.

Why else did the Home Secretary address the following memorandum to all Chief Constables March of 1957?

1   What is the number of coloured people in your area. a. West Indians and b. Non–West Indians?
2   Is there any definite evidence of large scale crime?
3   Do they mix well with white people?
4   What are the facts of illegitimacy related to West Indians?

5   What is the evidence concerning brothel management and coloured people?
6   What are the conditions under which they live?

This notion of blacks as loose in morals informed the Home Secretary's memorandum. It is not difficult to imagine the howls of protest from all quarters should the police be detailed to investigate the white population in this way.

Nothing in our view could so guarantee continued police malpractice within the black community as the carte blanche given to officers to investigate the six points outlined by the Home Secretary. Do they dare tell us that scores of Police Constables, with clapper board at hand, were mobilised to make discreet door to door surveys at West Indian occupied homes?

Quite the opposite actually too place. It was in this atmosphere that the term 'nigger hunting' was coined. Listen to the report prepared by the West Indian Standing Conference:

It has been confirmed that Sergeants and Constables do leave stations with the express purpose of going 'nigger hunting', that is to say, they do not get orders to act in this way, but among themselves they decide to bring in a coloured person at all cost.

The Standing Conference comprised of men and women brought up on a diet of British democracy as the ideal system, could be excused for their naiveté. It was beyond them at the time to grasp that a British Home Secretary would sanction 'nigger hunting'.

The report goes on to describe the modus operandi:

The difficulty to apprehend the policemen who indulge in these hunts, lies in the fact most of them go out in plain clothes, they use their own cars and in many instances, persons who are threatened or assaulted cannot get their numbers. Even when a coloured man

attempts to take a policeman's number he is appre-
hended for obstruction.

The black suspect must have lived in a constant state of
bewilderment at the line of questioning employed by officers
at police stations:

"How many rooms are there in your house?"
"Who sleeps where?"
"Have you got a separate kitchen and bath?"
"Are your children legitimate?"
"Does the woman in the flat above have many male
    visitors?"
"Do you say good morning to Mr and Mrs Smith who live
    next door?"
"Why not?"

The arrogance, the sheer confidence with which officers
framed blacks and executed physical brutality was drawn from
the unbridled power derived from Home Office and the media
which fawned over every comment from the police.

It is this image of crime and vice which provoked the
broadening of the crusade to involve white citizens in physical
attacks on blacks.

In October 1958 the Home Secretary proclaimed to the
nation, about the Notting Hill Race Riots, that "difficulties arose
partly through vice". Armed with that statement, 'nigger hunting'
as a police practice was signed, sealed and delivered. To this
day neither the Home Office nor the police have advanced any
evidence that the black population was ever, to any substantial
degree, involved in large scale vice activity. And where these
small clubs emerged, it was due to the failure of those who ruled
and governed to sanction and appreciate the self–creativity of
the black population in generating institutions of their own.

It was in the course of these weekend engagements that
the British policeman was himself transformed. From Bobby to
Babylon.

Only the most dyed-in-the wool racist would fail to foresee that the black working class in Britain, like its white counter-part, would embark on a struggle aimed at returning the British police to its proper place; aimed at driving the British police from the threshold of the black home; aimed at establishing the West Indian's home as his castle.

Two elements served as constraints on the West Indian community. Firstly, our very presence in Britain was as a result of the defeat of the Caribbean working class in the pre and post Second World War anti-colonial movements. The defeated and demoralised must necessarily experience a period of caution before traditions of rebellion are rekindled. And secondly, we were constrained by the fact that we were a minority and could not guarantee what whites would do in any major struggles against the police. White attitudes ranged then from the crude racialism, popular among large sections of the white working classes, to a finely honed racialism of the white and liberal left which blamed all on our persistent adherence to strange cultural practices, and a failure to integrate into the main-stream of the British way of life.

The West Indian population did not, however, come alive in Britain. Centuries of struggles — riots, strikes, insurrections, social campaigns — helped to shape a population, which had experienced a brutal slave and colonial past.

We had, immediately prior to mass immigration into Britain, fought bitter struggles against the colonial office to establish an organised labour movement, independent trade unions, in many cases accompanied by political parties of organised labour, which proliferated in almost every Carib-bean territory. Where the local police and militia were unable to cope, the armed might of the British army and navy threat-ened. And we were well versed in the struggle against police brutality and corruption. The author well remembers the oft-quoted incident involving a Trinidadian police officer, Charlie King. He was much hated by the Trinidadian oil workers for his brutal exercise of colonial power. In the heat of an oil strike he was cornered by striking oil workers, given a petrol bath and set on fire.

It would take much more than the British police to reduce such a population into a weeping, whimpering mass of defenceless workers.

Even with the constraints described, the police were able to detect elements of resistance and opposition. Chief Superintendent JR Norman, based at Scotland Yard, expressed the view that the police were becoming indignant because of constant challenges being made on them by West Indians. Norman continued that this phenomenon was a strange feature, for whereas a white man would humbly acquiesce to an order of a police officer, the West Indian would question it.

With this attitude and practice prevailing, such currents as existed in the black community would necessarily find organisational form and expression. In September 1958, the Coloured People's Progressive Organisation emerged under the leadership of Frances Ezzreco and George David. They demanded, at once, that "action should be taken against any police discrimination". The Committee for African Organisation protested to Prime Minister Macmillan that "coloured citizens in the UK have lost confidence in the ability of law enforcement agencies to protect them".

Nor was the resistance solely confined to the police. For the first time blacks in Britain would be educated en masse about the much touted impartiality of the legal system. A British lawyer has told us, in conversation, that he was being bombarded, week after week, with cases arising from the weekend raids on house parties. He admits his training guided him to advise his clients to plead guilty in those cases where the evidence, on the face of it, appeared to lead to a conviction. His seniors drilled into him the pact which exists between the practitioner and the court, to reduce to a minimum the number of contested cases. Whenever he approached his West Indian clients, they, in most cases, vehemently refused: 'Whatever the price I have to pay, I am pleading not guilty, go in there and defend me,' they would say. And he did. There were others, referred to in the black community as police lawyers, in whose way the police pushed cases. In return they would collude with police officers in securing their own client's conviction.

Invariably, the magistrates would rubber stamp police evidence, but the rebellious spirit of the black community could not be suppressed. Later, blacks were to organise groups of lawyers who would be on call for 24 hours and, of the greatest importance, who would follow client's instructions to the letter. 'Defence' was set up in Notting Hill with the assistance of the celebrated author, Colin MacInnes. Then the West Indian Standing Conference set up a panel of lawyers for similar purposes.

It may be of some surprise to those who are presently engaged in the current campaign to abolish the 'sus' law that 'nigger hunters' of the mid and late sixties had resurrected, from the cobwebs of legal antiquity, the vague and nebulous accusation of 'loitering with intent'. The charge became the stock-in-trade of police officers in North London, Notting Hill and Brixton.

There is, in circumstances of oppression, never a clear and clean line between those who rebel and those who don't. Avenues are always created by the victims through which direct confrontation or principled resistance are avoided. Sections of the West Indian population sought coldly and deliberately to draw police officers into a cesspool of corruption. Owners of illegal clubs, popularly called 'shebeens' and gaming houses were a source of 'earners' for police officers. The swift exchange of pound notes provided insurance against constant raids and harassment. The pimp, the gambler and the illegal alcohol vendor had encircled police officers in a web of corruption.

And the police denied it all. Whatever difficulties there were stemmed from a lack of understanding of modern police procedures on the part of the new immigrant. The Brixton police offered the West Indian Standing Conference the following explanation for the deteriorating relations between blacks and the police:

> The new Lambethans have found themselves entangled in the complexity of a highly industrialised society.

Nothing could be further from the truth. Caribbean peoples, like their British counterparts, were saddled with modern policing from time immemorial. Like our British counterparts, we have had to struggle to keep West Indian policemen in their proper place, sometimes with a violence equal in intensity to anything in the British Isles.

The Brixton police were fortunate that the new Lambethans did not revive some of our traditions on the streets of Brixton. We understood modern policing only too well.

And in stepped Detective Sergeant Challenor to demonstrate what modern policing in a highly industrial society was all about. He was stationed at the West End Central police station. Vigilant counsel had exposed him as having planted a half brick on one of the demonstrators at a rally mobilised to protest about the political events in Greece.

There then followed a procession of defendants who had to be pardoned, some released from custody on frame-ups which ranged from the planting of a jemmy, detonator caps, cigarette lighters, offensive weapons and half bricks, in an orgy of fabricated evidence. The famous line to emerge from that whole investigation was coined by Challenor as he vigorously pursued his enquiries in relation to a black suspect. With folded fist, he unleashed a barrage of punches at the suspect, all the while singing this refrain: "Bongo, Bongo, Go back to the jungle".

Challenor ought to have served a long stretch at Her Majesty's pleasure. It would have meant vindication of the protests raised by the black population; it would have undermined the vulgar propaganda centred around the British bobby; it would have revealed that right here in the heart of the capital, under the noses of senior police officers, the most damnable police corruption prevailed.

Official society had to find a way out of this embarrassment, organise a cover up if you like. Junior officers were imprisoned and, on 16 September 1963, Detective Sergeant Challenor was suddenly declared medically unfit for duty and seven weeks later certified a paranoid schizophrenic. Only a madman, they seemed to be saying, could or would behave in such a way. Challenor was, within months, declared sane, eventually to be offered a comfortable sinecure in the growing industry of private security — the final resting place for corrupt officers.

Henceforth, we were treated to a remarkable juggling act. Officials at the Home Office coined the rotten apple theory for the single corrupt officer, no longer the platitudes about immigrants entangled in a highly industrialised society, but the one rotten apple in a barrel of the finest Coxs.

Urgent though the issues were, the black population faced formidable opposition in wringing any fundamental concession from the British establishment. We were up against the persistent myth of the British bobby; a police force which pushed its propaganda to the white population through an accommodating media; a government which demanded that the black population, as new immigrants, be whipped into shape in order to facilitate the accumulation of international capital; a legal system which, for centuries, had paraded its impartiality before the world; a political left which insisted that, though things were slightly amiss, it was our fault that we did not integrate; and the hostility of the white working classes, now driven into frenzied attacks on their black brothers and sisters as competition for the crumbs of capitalism intensified.

By the mid sixties, some crumbs were thrown our way. The Police Act 1964 included some of the recommendations made by the 1962 Commission of Enquiry. We were propagandised that the most far reaching, revolutionary concept was now enshrined in law. Section 49 (1) states:

Where the chief officer of police for any area receives a complaint from a member of the public against a member of the police force for that area he shall (unless the complaint alleges an offence with which the member of the police force has been charged) forthwith record the complaint and cause it to be investigated and for that purpose may and shall if directed by the Secretary of State, request the chief officer of police for any other police to provide an officer of the police force for that area to carry out an investigation.

Also, in January 1964, Lord Chief Justice Parker established a set of rules, the Judges' Rules, which offered safeguards to suspects held at police stations. Having satisfied itself that the leash on the police was strengthened, official society relaxed in a glow of self–satisfaction.

Stalemate. Nothing was resolved as we entered the latter half of the 1960s. Police officer investigated police officer and with monotonous regularity the notice was returned, 'no grounds for taking any action'. At the slightest criticism, officers would waive the complaints system as a foolproof source of redress. The system was tested by blacks from John O'Groats to Lands End. And only recently we were told by a Chief Constable that the complaints system was being abused by trouble makers.

Black Power march, Lancaster Road, West London, 1970

Cause For Concern
In the Public Eye

Until the summer of 1968, the corruption and brutality visited on the black community by the police, and the resentment and hostility which police malpractice had generated among blacks, remained largely privatised and ghettoised.

One could still, in those days, encounter blacks who would recoil in disbelief when told of the experiences of others at the hands of the police. 'No British bobby would behave in such a way,' they seemed to be saying. Or perhaps a look of total incredulity would greet complaints of police malpractice. Among whites it was not an issue at all. They had heard nothing and knew even less.

The strategy employed by black and multiracial groups served to reinforce this privatisation of our experiences. It was based on the view that a liberal section of the British ruling classes could be mobilised to use their power to ameliorate the colonial conditions under which we lived. Blacks were helpless victims whom the liberals, with black middle class aspirants alongside them, would assist in adjusting to the discipline and control of capitalist institutions. It meant tea and sympathy meetings with Chief Superintendent Norman and others of his ilk who were appointed to liaise with white liberals and blacks on matters of 'difficulties' with police officers. It meant activating the interest of this or that Member of Parliament, or the House of Lords, who had distinguished himself as having anti–colonial sentiments and who would perhaps whisper in the ear of the Home Secretary in extreme cases. What had to be avoided at all costs was the airing of this issue in public which would inevitably unleash the power of working class blacks, through which whites would be educated and forced to take a position.

Those of us who kept plugging for a public debate, as a precondition for unleashing the power of working class blacks, were to experience success in the most unlikely quarter. A BBC producer had been introduced to this area of the black experience and was moved to produce a documentary in the popular series 'Cause for Concern'. The series aimed to air those serious issues which affected sections of the population in the United Kingdom. A live discussion followed each documentary. The contents of this documentary were bold and unambiguous. Victims of police malpractice would be seen and heard offering dramatic revelations which were to be signed, sealed and delivered by an ex–police officer who had agreed to appear on the programme to detail his experiences at Chelsea police station in London. The first 20 seconds of the documentary illustrated a case of police brutality against a white building–worker, included perhaps to show that black and white suffered alike. There then followed other cases, all involving blacks, which would reveal to millions of viewers that the police physically brutalised blacks, framed us on trumped up charges and fabricated evidence to secure criminal convictions.

The viewing public heard from a schoolteacher that he and his friend, a barrister, had been planted with car keys and charged with attempting to steal a motor car. They were found not guilty and a sum of £8,000 damages was awarded against the Metropolitan police. We were treated to another case of a young black worker who was arrested on a 'sus' charge. The defendant could provide evidence that he was at work when the police claimed that they were observing him dipping into handbags with intent to steal.

There were a few more fine treats but none greater than the ex–police officer who told all. No need to paraphrase him. Here it is, just as he told it:

Ex–policeman: Well I think in the police force you find a complex of prejudiced minorities. For example you might find that a certain number of police officers would be prejudiced against taxi drivers, bus drivers or against Jewish people. But I think that colour prejudice is virtually absolute. In other words it extends to probably 99%.

Interviewer: What efforts were made by senior officers to counteract it?

Ex–policeman: None at all that were apparent. Either they were unaware that it exists or they just chose to ignore it.

Interviewer: Amongst yourselves when you talked about coloured people — what was the general attitude?

Ex–policeman: I suppose one of looking on them as inferior people.

Interviewer: What sort of pressures are there on a policeman if he wants to do well at the job?

Ex–policeman: Well there is this sort of hardman cult which exists among the lower ranks and this required a young man to prove himself in many ways. Mainly it requires him to prove himself by the number of arrests he makes.

Interviewer: What about this in relation to coloured people. Are they more vulnerable?

Ex–policeman: The old tradition would be that the coloured man is not as fully aware of his rights as a white man would be and on this assumption I suppose he would be more vulnerable.

Interviewer: How did you feel about it?

Ex–policeman: Well it's very difficult to preserve any individual views that one might have had at the outset. It's uh you get carried along with the tide.

Interviewer: Did you ever feel like objecting?

Ex–policeman: Well naturally, one feels like objecting; I don't know; I can't speak for everyone, but I felt like objecting on a few occasions, but it would have been out of the question. It would have been socially unacceptable within the police force.

The screening of the 'Cause for Concern' programme turned out to be a major watershed in the struggle in which the police and the black community were locked. A conspiracy of silence had kept the issue from public view, thereby reinforcing the untrammelled power exercised by the police over the black community. The screening of the programme would surely alter the balance of power in this all–important struggle.

Once the police establishment discovered what the contents of the film were to be, they set in motion a series of desperate manoeuvres aimed at keeping it out of the public view. It is worth recording these in some detail.

Robert Mark, the then Deputy Commissioner of the Metropolitan Police, describes in his autobiographical tract, 'In the Office of Constable', the atmosphere at Scotland Yard:

Representatives of the Met were only allowed to see the film after its completion. They were horrified. The

Commissioner objected to its viewing and the BBC got cold feet. Then course of the civil libertarian press began to rage about censorship and, to make matters worse the Commissioner gave a brief interview to ITV. The BBC therefore decided to go head.

Mark's record conceals more than it reveals. It was not simply a case of the Commissioner objecting. Senior officers at Scotland yard, with a legal minion in tow, issued every conceivable threat against BBC staff. They were ready to withdraw any future co-operation with BBC journalists; they threatened to invoke the might of the civil law as talk about injunctions flew thick and fast. The BBC management bowed to police pressure and the film was withdrawn from the air.

What Mark described as the civil libertarian press was not the only force hot on the heels of the BBC. The story broke in the national press as an anti-censorship lobby swung into action. A picket was mounted at the BBC's Lime Grove Studios. The police reacted viciously and indicated that they would sink to any depths in their determination to keep the issue away from the public. They at once arrested Black Power activist, Obi Egbuna, on a charge of uttering and writing threats to kill police officers at Hyde Park, and with the trumpeters of Fleet Street in full attendance, the police were now made out to be on the defensive against a black, murderous fanaticism. The screening of such a programme in the present atmosphere, argued the Commissioner on the opposite television channel, would stir up fanatical passions and indeed, with Egbuna's trial outstanding, the screening of the programme would violate the sub judice rule. It was a desperate legal bid but one easily squashed.

As public criticism threatened to develop into a crescendo, the BBC caved in. The documentary, and the discussion arranged to follow, was back on the scheduled list of programmes. All this took place in full view of the black community and the general public, thereby ensuring a formidable increase in the numbers who would view the programme. We were not to know, at least not at that point, that the police would not concede defeat.

The civilian participants in the live discussion arrived at the BBC studios, at Lime Grove, at least one hour before the discussion was scheduled to go on the air. We were hustled by nervous BBC officials into a small and airless hospitality room. Robert Mark, Ray Merricks from the Community Relations Branch at Scotland Yard and Reg Gale of the Police Federation were housed next door.

We, the civilian participants, were cock–a–hoop from our recent victory and exuded the confidence which victory generates. Only days before we were together on the picket line demanding that the BBC screen the film; we were part of the discussions which assessed the nature of the anti–censorship struggle into which we had been thrown. We were therefore sharp and on the alert for any manoeuvres which the opposition might set in motion. We were not to be disappointed. A BBC official crept into our room, cleared his throat nervously, and announced that there would be a minor alteration in the arrangements for the live discussion. On the particular case which involved the white building-worker, the film omitted to mention that the building-worker had twice been convicted for carrying offensive weapons and that a City of London policemen had received £100 from the Criminal Injuries Board arising from his last arrest. And so, said the nervous official, the police would like to produce, as a witness, the officer who had received compensation. The witness would be examined and cross examined by the BBC presenter and ourselves.

Confronted by the fact that the examination of the police officer, his questioning and cross questioning, would exhaust the time allotted for the discussion, we asked the BBC official to leave the room so that we might consider the proposal.

It was clear that the police wished to avoid any discussion on the central question of what they were doing to blacks.

Mark again describes the atmosphere from which this latest manoeuvre sprung:

> "Clearly we had to be represented in the subsequent discussion and there were no volunteers. The day before it was due to be shown, the Commissioner told me that since I had more television experience than anyone else in the Met, I was to do it. I had no illusions about the task or about the good wishes I took with me."

The police reinforced their latest manoeuvre with a reckless alternative. If they did not get their way, they would not participate.

We emerged from our cabal with the firm but polite response that we did not wish to enter into any debate about the white building worker. We were there to discuss matters concerning blacks and the issue of the white worker was peripheral to this exercise. We were prepared to go on the air nevertheless. Neither the BBC, nor the police, were told what our trump card would be. We decided to continue the struggle to have the witness removed in full view of the millions who had tuned into the programme. We would expose the history of police attempts to have the film banned and their latest manoeuvre would be explained in that context. Should they persist with their demand, we would walk out of the studios at a pre–arranged signal. In all this we were guided by the fact that we knew the black community to be ready, and willing to engage official society in an uncompromising struggle to break out from the stranglehold of our isolation. We went on the air, with the embarrassed BBC presenter attempting in vain to mediate between the warring factions. The police persisted with their demand. "The witness had to appear. We will have every opportunity to cross–examine him and the public would be the final arbiters."

The signal was given, and as we moved to stage the walkout, publicly announcing what we were about to do, Reg Gale of the Police Federation relented. Thereafter, point after point went in our favour, once we had established that the police were down to the bottom of the barrel as they sought reasons to avoid the major issues.

Two clear positions emerged finally from this public debate. The police refused to accept the all pervasiveness of police oppression in the black community. The cases portrayed in the documentary were really isolated incidents created by a minority of rotten apples which any police force was bound to contain. And against these recalcitrant elements, the black community was well protected by the complaints system. The victim had only to lodge his complaint at a local police station to set in motion impartial police officers who would investigate the incident and justice would prevail. After all, they emphasised, the British police were the best in the world.

The black participants scotched the rotten apple theory. Police brutality and corruption were rampant inside the black community and the complaints system, with police investigating police, was a mere sham, producing the ritual reply that allegations against this or that police officer were not proven. One of the black activists rounded off his contribution with a clearly stated position: "The police must stop framing and brutalising blacks or the black community will organise to stop them." The success of the programme (both the film and the discussion) and the victory over attempts by the police to suppress the programme had important consequences for the struggle being waged by the black community to throw the burden of police oppression off our backs, and to exercise control and discipline over a police force, the members of which are our servants.

The fact that the film was shown at all, bold and unambiguous as the contents were, would strengthen the belief in the black community that the police armour could be penetrated and that they were not the invincible power they appeared to be. In short, they could be taken on and defeated. This would give tremendous strength and confidence to the movement.

Secondly, the struggle would no longer be conducted in

isolation from the rest of society. Once our experiences at the hands of the British police had crashed into public view, the black movement against police oppression could assess who our friends and enemies were and what hurdles had to be overcome. Immediately following the programme, the popular left journal, *Black Dwarf*, would carry a full transcript of the film and discussion. The doubting Thomases in the black community would be jolted out of their complacency and the process through which whites would be educated on an issue of crucial importance to black citizens would be set in motion.

And thirdly, the veil of impartiality would be torn from the image of the British police. They were seen to be recalcitrant in their refusal to accept and do anything about the all pervasiveness of their malpractices. And we were in no doubt, none whatever, that the police took such a rigid and hard position because they were certain of the support of politicians and large sections of the established press.

This changed balance of forces would play havoc with those black and multi–racial groups whose very existence served to fortify, within the black community, that our weakness was as such that no other approach but 'the whisper in the ear of authority' was possible.

How were we now to proceed became the central question which increasingly dominated this particular struggle. This begged the subsidiary question as to the reasons why the British police were behaving in this way towards blacks. The answers would reveal two political attitudes which would develop into major tendencies inside the black struggle as the rebellion of black workers against police oppression became a feature of national politics.

There was one tendency which could be described as nationalist. They were adamant that Britain was a racist society and it flowed from this that white police officers would themselves be racialists. Police officers allowed this subjective emotion to cloud their judgements and behaviour towards blacks. It would follow, equally, that this tendency would call for the elimination of racialism from within the police force. They would aim to restructure police training to include courses on the cultures of blacks; they would participate en masse in the race relations industry through which a gentle and polite dialogue would be held with police liaison officers from the community relations departments of the respective forces; they would call for black police officers. They were dominated by the ideological position that the black working class was powerless and would always remain so. The white working class was irretrievably racist and no alliance with them was possible. We had to unite with that section of British society which had the power — the liberal section of the ruling class.

The Campaign Against Racial Discrimination, a mere carcass by then, and the small islandic groupings, which displayed such sparkle and energy in assisting the newly arrived West Indians in making the social and cultural adjustments on this strange and hostile terrain, could not see beyond racialism and would now become irrevocably part of the status quo. Leading personnel in these organisations were induced to apply for jobs in the state-controlled race relations industry. Those who had distinguished themselves in the subtleties of whispering were appointed to overlord the race relations bureaucracy.

The other tendency, the radical tendency, would accept that the police force was replete with racist sentiments; but that was not the fundamental cause by any means. The fundamental reason, we argued turned on the fact that the black community had to be disciplined and organised to produce wealth at little cost to the capitalists. The discipline and obedience required were not only confined to the factory but had to be extended throughout all areas of our social lives. The foremen at our various places of work would ensure that we performed as was necessary, and the police were on the front line in seeing to it that we went about our social lives in the strait-jacket required for the obedient worker. Any deviation from the norm would necessitate stringent action. To be unemployed and on the streets means that we were not being productive. The original charge of loitering with intent, 'sus', would involve the magistracy and prison officers in whipping us back into line. Late night parties, shebeens, carnival festivals et al would disrupt the smooth rhythm of the working day and therefore had to be harassed out of existence. The fact that police officers were racialist would greatly assist capital in exercising the harshest of disciplines over this new workforce.

Every conceivable colonial myth would be regurgitated to justify what the police were doing. We were basically lazy and slothful, prone to vice, crime and Bacchanalian activity. At the slightest opportunity, we would opt for not working at all. It had to be the British police who would ensure that we produced the surplus value required for British capitalism's post–war survival.

Jim Callaghan, then an ordinary Member of Parliament, described our purpose with precision:

> Every immigrant represents a store of capital. It costs £4,000 to raise, educate and train a person for productive employment and this sum is transferred as a free export wherever immigration takes place... Britain, with full employment, and an immense programme of rebuilding to be tackled, needs immigrants urgently. We have a population of 50 million, a working population of 25 million, and it is this productive group that feeds and clothes and shelters all our children and pensioners. Each new immigrant at work helps provide for the unproductive half of the population. Ask the Germans how they managed to win prosperity from the shambles of 1945. Hard work? Yes. But with a labour force strengthened by millions of immigrants. Germany lost the war and was paid reparations in human capital.

For us the only countervailing power capable of releasing the black community form this exercise of state power was the black working class, human capital, unified, disciplined and organised by the very mechanism of capitalist production. We viewed the mass rebellion of the black working class as inevitable and it was only through such a rebellion, skilfully orchestrated and organised, that the white working class could be set in motion.

The clash between these two tendencies inside the black struggle would become even sharper because of the profound changes in composition and consequently in the consciousness of the West Indian population. Thousands of young blacks, who were either born in Britain or who had grown up on native soil, were now entering the labour market with expectations nurtured in the schooling system. They ate school dinners with the same ease as their white counterparts, passed or failed the same examinations, suffered equally the bankrupt ritual that passes for education in these parts. Their expectations were identical to those of young whites.

And what were they offered? These young blacks were to discover that the buyers of labour power required them to be channelled into those jobs which their parents had no alternative but to accept. Their white counterparts would enter the world of apprenticeships which their parents had secured through the generations. The trades were the preserve of the white elite. The unskilled, deadly boring and repetitive work, distinguishable by its unsocial hours, would be the preserve of blacks.

And how they rebelled! En masse, young blacks refused to follow their parents into these jobs. By their rebellion, they created a shortage of labour in certain areas of the economy. They offered little or no competition to the older generation. No queues could be found outside the factories and the recruiting offices of the service industries as obtained in the late fifties and early sixties. The older blacks could successfully unleash a torrent of industrial struggles for increased wages and better working conditions without any fear of being replaced by willing school leavers.

Some of the youth took what jobs were available but their employers found them to be quite a different kettle of fish from their parents. This force of young blacks was free from the constraints which kept the older generation at heel. Firstly, they were free, and still remain so, from any experience of class demoralisation and defeat. Secondly, they were socialised in large numbers in classrooms alongside white, working class youth and therefore had a better measure than did their parents of how whites would respond to concerted black mobilisation on any of the issues we were up against. And thirdly they were free from the inhibiting myth that sooner or later they would return to their native land. For them Britain is home.

The development of young blacks inside British capitalism rendered them incompatible with the social arrangements they had inherited.

This new presence in the social and political life of the black community would dissipate any lingering doubts that the Labour Party would be the political vehicle for black working class emancipation.

And the organisational and theoretical impasse had to be broken. It was a matter of extreme urgency since the police, having established their unbridled power in the 1950s and 1960s, turned their undivided attention to the rebellious young blacks. The 'sus' weapon, so finely perfected in the earlier period, would be unleashed without mercy. The police, now armed with the powers of stop and search under the Misuse of Drugs Act, sought out the black youth who were easily identifiable targets. The reggae culture brought together hundreds of youths at a time in youth clubs all over the country, and the police would storm these institutions in the same manner as they did the homes of West Indians in the earlier period.

The organisational question would now be resolved by another section in the vast industrial army of international black labour. The American section of this international army of black labour would harass, tease and taunt the American power structure from the late sixties and for a decade after with the slogan 'Black Power'. Under the banner, the theory of independent black working class radical organisation would be teased out.

Stokely Carmichael followed Martin Luther King and Malcolm X to Britain to lay down, at a conference entitled 'The Dialectics of Liberation', the basic thinking and experience behind the slogan 'Black Power'. It was this event, coupled with the unceasing flow if literature from North America, which would break the impasse, to which the social movement, with particular concerns about police oppression, had succumbed.

The theory and philosophy of 'Black Power' would answer the questions, some fully and other partially, so urgently posed in the late sixties.

Young blacks organised themselves into Black Power groups throughout the country, linking North, Midlands and South in a national movement. Though a small minority actually joined organisations, the existing political ethos was dominated by the philosophy and political perspective of 'Black Power'. The older West Indians were, by and large, absent from mass gatherings and political activism. They offered their sympathy and support, moderated by some reservations at the boldness and audacity of this new force. Political movements of some significance always announce themselves with this uneasy balance between different sections of the class or social groupings involved.

Heading the agenda of every one of these organisations' programmes was the issue of police oppression in the black community. There resided in the Black Power organisations and the campaigns they fought an uneasy alliance between the nationalist and the radical tendencies.

By the summer of 1970 young blacks were in open rebellion, encouraged by and drawing strength from what others were doing and acting on in other areas of British society and in different theatres on the international scene. Strikes and shop floor rebellions among older black workers moved the journal *British Industry Week* 6 June, 1969, to comment:

As another troubled summer starts in the US, employers there are getting worried. Worried about the rising influence of the Black Power Movement in industry. In the motor industry there the revolutionary fervour of black militants is high. . . Already there have been signs that Britain's coloured labour is capable of militancy.

(The phrase 'is capable' remains instructive. The entire British economy was run on the assumption that we weren't.) Homeless white workers plagued local councils with a squatting movement in which thousands seized empty housing stock in order to house themselves. An enormous rent strike engulfed East London and the trade unions were letting everyone know that a wage freeze would not be tolerated.

What was lacking on the home front would be adequately supplied in activity further afield. The Catholic working class in Northern Ireland had given notice that British oppression would be severely challenged; African peasants would resort to armed struggle to resist and finally overthrow Portuguese colonial oppression; the Black Panthers in the USA called the unemployed, urban poor to armed rebellion; de Gaulle hung on to power by his fingertips as all Europe shook under the weight of working class revolt. In the Caribbean, Trinidad in particular, workers and peasants were out on the streets. A helicopter stood by waiting to evacuate the Prime Minister, Eric Williams, after demonstrations and strikes all but toppled the regime. And the Vietnamese peasantry were well on their way to debunking the myth that the American power structure was invincible.

Young blacks, here in Britain, would lead the rebellion against police oppression sure in the belief that they were part of an international movement, rich in variety.

Street fighting erupted in North London between young blacks and the police, resulting in a few arrests. At the end of the day, the black youth stormed the Caledonian Road police station and demanded the release of those arrested. Hours later, we received news that Jonathan Jackson had walked into a California court, armed to the teeth, demanding the release of his brother George and other black prisoners.

Within two days, 300 blacks and a handful of white supporters presented themselves on the streets of Notting Hill there to demonstrate, with chilling effect, their opposition to attempts by the West London police to harass the Mangrove restaurant out of existence.

It was this event and the political trial which followed, that altered completely all the methods through which our struggles against the police and the courts had been conducted. It would lay down the guidelines which would haunt all future political activity on this score. In short, it was a historic event.

The Mangrove Restaurant was an attempt by the Trinidadian owner, Frank Crichlow, at providing an up–market West Indian cuisine in Notting Hill.

It was a development on the Rio Coffee Bar which he ran in the late fifties and early sixties. By then, Notting Hill had become a major area in which the new black immigrants had settled. Dotted throughout the community were small clubs and eating houses organised by West Indians for West Indians. It was on this terrain that the West Indian community fought off the white attackers in the Notting Hill riot of 1959.

The Rio Coffee Bar catered for the unemployed section of the West Indian community. The basement hosted a gambling club operated outside of the discipline of the Gaming Act. There were quite a number of these in the area. Some of the proprietors were forced into paying sums to the police so that they could operate freely; they provided the base from which pay offs were made to the police for the favour of not opposing bail for one of their clients; they facilitated contacts through which bribes were paid so that previous convictions would not be read out in court; they provided the habitation for the police penetration of the ganja trade. Frank Crichlow distinguished himself as an opponent of these practices. In fact he organised opposition to the police corruption and other excesses. Along with others, he pioneered the organisation 'Defence' with its headquarters at his home in Maida Vale.

'Defence', the precursor of 'Release', was formed when

Lennard Waithe, one of the Rio's clients, was sentenced to four years imprisonment on a trumped up charge of living off immoral earnings. The organisation aimed to provide legal advice and assistance to those victimised by the police. Henceforth, Frank's cuisine would be seasoned with a fair sprinkling of political action. He would be marked for future reference as a trouble maker with anti-police sentiments.

By the late 1960s, Notting Hill had welcomed a new addition of migrants. The sons and daughters of the international white middle classes, imbued with the heady mix of flower power, had set up communes and other radical institutions in the area. The Mangrove served up market soul food to this mixed clientele during the evenings and a black barrister was on hand throughout the day to train all his energies and skills on the Notting Hill, Notting Dale and Harrow Road police stations.

The presence of a barrister served as a major disruption to the well-rehearsed procedures for dealing with black suspects at these police stations. He fought successfully the lame and malicious opposition to bail. With the immediate presence of a lawyer at a police station, the chances of suspects making statements of admission under pressure were cut to a minimum; the time and space within which beatings could take place were greatly reduced. The police stood to lose both income and some of the weapons in their arsenal of oppression. The Mangrove had to go.

There developed, in every police station responsible for policing the black community, a group of policemen who had impressed their superiors and colleagues that they were proficient at handling blacks. Their names were familiar to most. The Notting Hill contingent was known as the heavy mob; spearheaded by a PC Pulley and included PCs Rogers, Lewis and Reid. These officers trained all their energies on the Mangrove and mobilised other officers to do the same. The mere mention of Pulley would strike terror in the hearts of blacks in Notting Hill. He strutted through the streets of Notting Hill, administering sharp doses of capitalist discipline, abjuring all legal procedure. He was the colonial governor reincarnate.

He led sortie after sortie into the Mangrove. There were three drug raids in six months backed by a deluge of residents' objections to the council's renewal of the all–night licence. The sheer concentration of all this activity in a six month period led all to believe that the residents' objections were prompted by the police. The raids produced no evidence of drugs on the premises, and the fact that we were all aware that nothing of the kind was obtained at the Mangrove, sharpened the urgency for action.

Frank Crichlow explored every avenue provided by official society but to no avail. Local MPs, the police complaints system, the Home Office, social workers, advice centres, even a member of the House of Lords. No redress. Frank discovered that there was nothing in official society to restrict the police from painting the Mangrove a den of iniquity, driving the clientele away, so as to restore their hegemony over the black community. Where official society failed to protect the Mangrove, the black community and our supporters would undertake the responsibility.

The Action Committee for the Defence of the Mangrove was formed, and in alliance with the Black Panther Movement, called a public demonstration of protest on 9 August, 1970. The following letter addressed to the Home Office, the Prime Minister, the Leader of the Opposition, the High Commissioners for Jamaica, Trinidad, Guyana, and Barbados announced the march:

> We the black people of London have called this demonstration in protest against police harassment which is being carried out against us, and which is condoned by the legal system. In particular, we are calling for an end to the persecution of the Mangrove Restaurant of 8, All Saints Road, a restaurant that serves the black community. These deliberate raids, harassments and provocations have been reported to the Home Office on many occasions. So too has the mounting list of grievances

such as raids on West Indian parties, wedding receptions and other places where black people lawfully gather.

We feel this protest is necessary as all other methods have failed to bring about any change in the manner the police have chosen to deal with black people. We shall continue to protest until black people are treated with justice by the police and law courts.

Signed,
Anthony Mohipp,
Barrister-at-Law,
Action Committee for the Defence of the Mangrove.

Polite but firm. Black Power it certainly was, perhaps tinged with a little British constitutionality. The Action Group would mobilise blacks on the streets of Notting Hill in declared opposition to years of unbridled police power.

Even the unpredictable British weather would come out in support of Black Power. Bright sunshine, tempered with the hint of a breeze. Just enough to draw a slight flutter from the flags, there to reveal the black panther uncoiled and ready to spring.

The crowd gathered, fitfully at first, before surrounding the first speaker who intoned from the makeshift platform — an abandoned vehicle parked immediately in front of the Mangrove:

We have complained to the police about the police and nothing has been done, we have complained to judges about judges and nothing has been done, we have complained to magistrates about magistrates and nothing has been done, we have complained to the council about the council and nothing has been done, now we have to do something ourselves.

It was a precise and correct political description of the stage reached by a movement which had, in the preceding 15 years, probed, prodded and appealed to official society to offer some redress on the vexed question of police oppression in the black community.

And official society responded on that day. A menacing force of hundreds of uniformed police officers, outnumbering the demonstrators two to one, hovered in the background as the demonstrators set off in the mid afternoon, hemmed in by hundreds of police officers, meat wagons, panda cars, photographic equipment in tow. A remarkable mobilisation of state violence. "The pigs, the pigs, we have got to get rid of the pigs." Chanted the crowd. They were on their way to pay visits to the three police stations which held the black community in the area in a state of siege. The flag of the Brixton–based Black Panther Movement fluttered at the head of the demonstration, introducing a slight hint of the militancy. Their placards were bold if a little unimaginative. 'Kill the Pigs', 'The Gun This Time', 'Hands off Black People' and Barbara Beese held a real pig's head aloft, an indication that perhaps decapitation might be a possible solution.

As we approached the Notting Dale police station, PC Pulley, against whom every nefarious deed was alleged, was identified: 'Pulley Must Go'.

Not one of us was unaware of an almost paralytic hostility coming from the hundreds of the police officers who surrounded us on that day. During the last leg of our long march, finally to be completed at Harrow Road police station, the inevitable took place. The demonstration literally exploded. The violence was ferocious, as the combatants continued, for 15 minutes, to batter, to wound and to maim each other. The police were moved to an orgy of violence and abuse. It was a street fight. Not one single officer entertained that much–touted skill of crowd control. It was pure, unadulterated, unlicensed brutality. The niggers were to be beaten into the ground. How dare we, they seemed to be saying, take to the streets in opposition to them? We did not qualify. Anybody but a bunch of niggers. Crude though the language may be, the words fittingly described the reaction of the British state on that day.

We gave as good as we got. Bricks, stones, bottles, any ammunition at hand, we threw at the police. Whole building skips were emptied at them.

On the following day, and for a full week afterwards, the national and international press focused on the demonstration. Apart from scattered, sympathetic responses, the press fed the British public a diet of worn out clichés about race relations, downright lies and political slander. Clearly identified were those Black Power agitators who had homed in on what they described as a simple and unsuspecting population. The Home Secretary called for an enquiry into Black Power and the *Daily Mirror*, of 11 August announced that "Special Branch files on known agitators in the field of race relations are being studied by Commander John Gerrard who is in charge of the Public Disorder department at Scotland Yard".

It was the police who fed the press and politicians the 'Black Power agitators' line and they willingly fed at the trough. The political police were mobilised to present a report to the Home Secretary. Subsequent events would reveal that the police distorted the information that they had gathered. All talk about the police as an impartial body is sheer baloney. For the police knew that on that day, assembled on the streets of Notting Hill were the veterans of the fifties who marched alongside young blacks. The veterans would bring to the march the experiences of the dark days when Ossie paid the police to keep his gambling house open; when they stood helplessly by whilst their homes and private functions were violated by police officers; when they found themselves powerless to respond as Lennard Waithe was arrested by police, and imprisoned on a frame–up charge of living off immoral earnings; when PC Pulley ruled the roost; when only the favourites of the police were allowed to run shebeens and sell ganja. All history jelled that day. And the youths had their grievances too. They were being sussed left, right and centre, no youth club was safe from police intruders.

They were stopped and searched willy-nilly at the whim of any racist officer now given licence under the Misuse of Drugs Act.

The truth of the matter was that a section of the British working class, distinguishable by the colour of our skins, had declared open rebellion against the British state. And the British state reacted in the same manner as it had done to generations of Irish, Scottish, Welsh and English workers.

Detective Inspector Stockwell, shy and retiring, but with an obsessive eye for detail, was charged with the responsibility for debriefing every single officer who attended the march. All hinged on the quartet of police officers, Pulley, Lewis, Reid and Rogers, (the heavy mob) who, throughout the march, spied on the demonstrators through the slits in a nondescript van. Stockwell and his team toured the working class community in Portnall Road where the fight took place. They were attempting to solicit statements from residents that the violence at the demonstration terrorised them. It is important here to note that not one single black resident would co-operate. Later, they would inform us that they believed the action taken by demonstrators to be justified. A section of whites did co-operate and from them came only the most faint-hearted admissions.

Stockwell's documentation, including photographs taken by the *Daily Mirror*'s photographer, was dutifully passed on to the Director of Public Prosecutions. Hitherto, unknown by the black community, the DPP would now assume a power and importance in full view of the black community. Behind this obscure figure hid an insidious political decision handed down from the Home Secretary. Those whom the official files deemed black agitators were extracted from the body of demonstrators and charged with indictments handed down from the DPP some 11 weeks later. The nine, all black, were charged with inciting members of the public to kill police officers, incitement to riot and causing an affray.

It was the whip of the counter revolution. Like their American counterparts, the British government would attempt to imprison those they deemed the political leaders and later dissipate the rebellious with a series of pacification measures.

The movement was tested now as it had never been before. We were faced with replying to Inspector Stockwell in the courts detail for detail, burdened as we were by the tendency among lawyers to compromise their clients. We had to match, with propaganda of our own, the vast machine which the British state would summon at its disposal. We had to combat the tendency of the British state to mobilise support among whites who belonged to the same social class as ourselves. We had to be on the alert for black middle class deals with state power.

There was much that we could draw on from our anti–colonial history to meet this challenge. Equally, the international arena was replete with revolutionary practice from which we could fashion a programme of activity. The loose alliance between the Action Group and the Black Panther Movement was the vehicle through which we attempted to execute these historical tasks and transcend the 'whisper in the ear of authority' approach. The defendants assumed a centrality in all these activities.

Althea Jones Lecointe was a Phd student, a leader of the Black Panther Movement and an offspring of the Trinidad lower middle classes; Rupert Boyce was disciplined by British Rail as a ticket collector; Barbara Beese, was born here, taught at a primary school and cared for her son and her home; Carlyle Inniss worked when he could and was prepared to raise money by means not sanctioned by law; Goffrey Millette sold his labour power on the market for the unskilled; Roddy Kentish, well into his thirties, freelanced as a motor mechanic; Rhoden Gordon gave as his discipline the pompous title race relations research worker; Frank Crichlow, a small business man, provided the catalyst through which a whole range of historical needs and emotions would be expressed; the author worked as a journalist and had recently returned from participating in the revolt which all but toppled Williams' regime in Trinidad.

On our side, actually and potentially, were the hundreds

of thousands of West Indians educated by experience, word of mouth and the scores of the Black Power leaflets which propagandised on this issue of police oppression; an Asian population with experiences of the exploitation and oppression all their own, the white British working classes with their concerns brought on by successive governments since the Second World War; and an international campaign drawing upon every inch of the tradition from a long and troubled anti-colonial history. By the time the trial was scheduled to begin the issues were placed before Caribbean peoples, blacks and whites throughout the United Kingdom. Support poured in from the black movement in the United States. The black community, at a massive rally in Notting Hill, gave the nine defendants a terrific send off on the day before we were to appear at the Old Bailey.

With a successful campaign behind us, the legal side had to be of the first order. We amassed a crew of lawyers who had distinguished themselves in matter pertaining to civil liberties. They were part of the liberal tradition inside the British establishment and carried in their baggage the much touted liberal compromise. We were having none of the deals, the guilty pleas in return for soft sentences, the give and take between defence and prosecution, the under the table exchanges of information all of which had plagued black defendants to date. We disabused the lawyers, at once, of any notion that they would be in charge of tactics and strategy during the trial. Those decisions would remain in the hands of the defendants who were in tune with the mood of our political constituency. We were prepared to take advice but final decisions would rest with the defendants. Two of the defendants chose to defend themselves, thereby releasing a section of the defence from the strict rigours of legal procedure. The defendants would meet daily for a month before the trial organising what our evidence would be, checking every detail of the prosecution's evidence. Very little was left to chance. In all of these preparations and during the trial itself we were strengthened by the unshakable loyalty and support of one of the barristers who received his education from black proletarians in those cruel days when the movement was smothered by those who could not see beyond whispering the ear of authority.

The trail began in October 1971 at the Old Bailey before Judge Clarke. He was notorious for his heavy sentencing and a right wing law and order approach to justice. Before a packed public gallery, we challenged for a jury of our peers, a black jury. Though this motion was not granted, the mere fact that we presented it at all served to establish that we were prepared to attack all the worn out and repressive bourgeois legal procedures. In motion after motion we raised the rights of the defendants for innumerable facilities. By the time the trial proper was scheduled to begin, we had amassed a bevy of black notetakers, a tape recorder of our own in the well of the court, and had won the right to have at our disposal a list of potential jurors and their occupations. Demonstrators thronged the picket line outside the Old Bailey if only to remind the British state that we had focused an international force on their judicial system. The feeling in the black community was electric. We had broken the stranglehold of lawyers on defendants and posed a powerful challenge to the legal system.

A jury of two blacks and 10 whites returned a majority of not guilty verdicts after 55 days, and when faced with sentencing the guilty on the minor charges, the heavy-handed judge was reduced to a whimper. This was the Xmas season, he mumbled, and he was prepared to extend to those defendants who were found guilty a measure of goodwill. No one was sent to prison. It was an enormous victory. Weeks later, 11 jurors dined at the Mangrove restaurant to celebrate our victory. They were apologetic about the guilty verdicts and generally hostile to the police. The British state could not convince whites to join them. Racism as a basis for the division of the working class took a beating, particularly since our defence was based on the fact that the police were liars and should not be believed.

Arrest, Brixton 1981. *Photo: John Sturrock.*

Brixton **Before The Riots**

The Metropolitan Police, London, in a confidential report on the uprising of young blacks in Brixton, recorded these grave historical facts:

> Between 6.10pm on Friday, 10 April, 1981, and 11.34pm on Monday, 13 April, 1981, during a very warm early spring interlude, serious disorder occurred in the immediate area of Brixton, SW9, within the Greater London Borough of Lambeth when large numbers of persons, predominantly black youths, attacked police, police vehicles (many of which were totally destroyed), attacked the Fire Brigade and damaged appliances, damaged private premises and vehicles, destroyed private premises and vehicles by fire, looted, ransacked and damaged shops, and there is one instance of a white girl being raped in her flat by a black youth whilst the disorder occurred around them. During the entire period some 7,472 police officers were used to police the area, some on more than one occasion.

The report goes on to inform that there were 285 arrests, 415 police officers and 172 members of the public injured,

118 police vehicles damaged, 4 police vehicles destroyed, 61 private vehicles damaged, 30 private vehicles destroyed, 158 premises damaged and 28 premises seriously damaged by fire.

Measured by any standards, this revolt assumed serious insurrectionary proportions. From Brixton the revolt snaked its way through Peckham, Southall, Wood Green, Finsbury Park, Woolwich, Forest Gate and Notting Hill in London; to Liverpool, Birkenhead, Sheffield, Manchester, Leeds, Hull, Newcastle and Preston in the North of England, taking in the Midland areas of Coventry, Leicester, Derby, Birmingham and Nottingham. And the South was affected too. Southampton, Cirencester, High Wycombe, Gloucester, Luton, Reading, Aldershot and Cardiff, all experienced the violent revolt of young blacks and whites against the police. The number of arrests, the extent of the damage to property and person were multiplied many times as British society saw no peace until the uprising petered out at the end of July 1981.

The period between 10 April and 23 July must be taken as a whole, distinguishable, as it was, in range and depth from previous revolts waged by blacks against the police. This general uprising stands head and shoulders above all that had gone before, and not simply in relation to the historical development of the black working class in Britain. Not since the insurrection of the 1830s — the Chartist Movement — has English society experienced such extensive revolt. Of equal importance is the fact that the uprising represents a massive leap from the late sixties and early seventies when young blacks combined under the Black Power banner to combat police violence and corruption inside the black community.

To investigate, as far as we can, what blacks did and how they did it during this period is to appraise ourselves of the stage that the black movement in Britain has reached and its impact on those sections of the society closest to us. In this way we are able to discover what is likely to develop in the coming period. To know is to be prepared.

It is convenient to isolate the Brixton uprising for our

purposes, precisely because much of what took place in other cities was contained in the Brixton revolt.

The revolt of Brixton's young blacks against the police did not begin when the media and the rest of British society discovered it on the weekend of 10 April to 13 April, 1981. In the last 10 years, young blacks in Brixton engaged the local police in minor skirmishes, organised protests, violent street confrontations and hand to hand fighting in youth clubs and other social haunts. Add to these the string of one to one incidents, characterised by the hostility and violent outbursts of the participants. Much of this history has taken place behind the backs of the rest of British society, often unrecorded except as a sensational one–off event. Recorded, they were, by the statisticians at Scotland Yard, but never as information from which others may arrive at objective analyses and recommendations, but always as vulgar propaganda aimed at bolstering up the image of the British police, always aimed at preparing public opinion for the introduction of, say, the Special Patrol Group in yet another assault on the black community. It is directly out of this history that the contending forces burst forth on the national and international stage on that fateful spring weekend in April 1981.

22 November, 1970, marked a significant turning point in this struggle. Joshua Francis worked at London Transport and lived in Brixton. On that day, in November 1970, the normal routine in the life of this middle–aged West Indian was brutally interrupted. Four white men, one of them an off duty police officer, stormed into his home and assaulted him, opening wounds which required 30 stitches. The Brixton police arrived, carted Mr Francis off to Brixton police station and charged him with assaulting three police officers. The attack on Joshua Francis was an unusual occurrence, the police reaction was not.

The West Indian community had, until then, developed a practice in dealing with experiences of this kind, a practice no different from that which obtained in society at large. They sought the advice of the local, voluntary organisation of their Islandic grouping, or the Citizens Advice Bureau, or maybe the local vicar who would, in turn, act as ushers to some local firm of solicitors. If not, they walked into a legal firm on the High Street or were touted for a firm of solicitors in the corridors of the Magistrates Court. The touts were mainly police officers who, it has been alleged, received 'backhanders' for their recommendations and were ensured co–operation in convicting the defendants. The radical lawyer, black or white, with the inclination to challenge police evidence, did not exist then. Convictions came thick and fast, hastened by the tendency among magistrates to rubber stamp police evidence. The most extreme action undertaken by the West Indian community entailed a complaint to the local Member of Parliament or to Scotland Yard. Such complaints invariably came to nothing. We lived that way for close to 15 years, overwhelmed by the weight of tradition that the British police were the best in the world and suffocated by institutions whose instincts were to reproduce that tradition.

Joshua Francis broke away, and assisting him a new course were members of the Black Panthers Movement, based in Brixton. Young blacks in Brixton had, a couple of years earlier, formed themselves into the Black Panther Movement. The membership was overwhelmingly working class with a sprinkling of intellectuals. At their height, the Panthers numbered close to 300 active members. They declared themselves opposed to police malpractice and published a newspaper which reflected a militant stance on this question. The paper was distributed from door to door in Brixton and the main shopping centre to which flocked black Brixtonians and other blacks from the surrounding South London black community. The Panthers held public meetings, sold radical and revolutionary literature, demonstrated and agitated in an effort to mobilise public vigilance and alertness with regard to the Brixton police. They demanded too, that arrested blacks be tried by a jury of their peers.

Nor was their platform that narrow. They drew up the battle lines on the education and housing fronts; they placed the struggles of Africans against Portuguese colonialism before the local community; they mobilised in support of Caribbean liberation struggles; they hoisted their banners on the Irish civil rights demonstrations; they were solid, they said, in their support for the Palestinian liberation struggles. Internally, they debated the pitfalls of nationalism and teased at Marxism and its various Chinese interpretations. It was a movement, distinguishable from previous forms by its radical vibrancy.

But the central issue remained the malpractices carried out against Brixton's black community by the police. On this score, the Panthers introduced the local black community to an alternative to the barren and bankrupt approaches which characterised the preceding period.

Joshua Francis placed his case in the hands of the Panthers, and they at once set about organising a campaign on his behalf. It was, perhaps, one of the first of such campaigns recorded in the history of the struggles between blacks and the Brixton police.

Freedom News, the journal of the Black Panther Movement, recorded the events as follows:

> Since the attack on the life of Brother Joshua Francis, the Black Panther Movement has been organising a campaign to involve the community in demanding justice for Brother Joshua and *an inquiry into the activities of the Brixton police, who have been allowed to mount these attacks on black people* (my emphasis).

Freedom News linked two similar events to illustrate the point:

> In 1967 a Brother Campbell was dragged from a bus on Brixton Road and beaten unconscious in broad daylight.

And again:

> In November 1969, three brothers and a sister were

again beaten, one of them (Bro Tex) received a broken arm: Black people in the (Brixton) market were protesting against an unwarranted attack on a Nigerian diplomat.

Later on, the journal drew our attention to the attitude of the judiciary and Joshua Francis' lawyer.

These criminal activities of the police have again been upheld with the conviction of Bro Joshua whose defence lawyer refused to raise the political issues involved in the case. The response of one barrister to a request by Joshua to have black people on the jury was met with the question, 'Are you mad?'

The campaign involved pickets of the courts, a public demonstration, public meetings and the publication and dissemination of reams of leaflets. All Brixton knew about Joshua Francis' case. All Brixton, black and white, was being introduced to a new and radical approach to a long standing problem. The responses were by no means uniform. Young blacks were unreservedly for this new approach, older West Indian workers expressed a cautious wait–and–see attitude, while offering a reserved sympathy. Working class whites were in the main sceptical, but by no means unalterably opposed. This approach was not confined to Brixton. In almost every black community in the country, groups emerged using the Panther organisation as a model.

These organisations of the Black Power period coalesced into a national formation at the National Conference on the Rights of Black People held in the spring of 1971 at Alexandra Palace. More than 800 representatives of the different organisations were present. The movement had reached its peak after a period of five to six years.

A combination of a black movement in its formative stages and the rise of Powellism prompted Harold Wilson, then Prime

Minister, to make the following remarks during a speech on the steps of Birmingham Town Hall on 5 May, 1968:

> That tragic and intractable phenomenon which we watched with horror on the other side of the Atlantic (burning cities in the USA) but which there is interwoven with history and existence of the States itself, is coming upon us here by our own volition and our own neglect. Indeed, it has all but come. In numerical terms, it will be of American proportions long before the end of the century.

Later on in 1971, the black movement, now at its peak and with a massive youth following, Harold Wilson again intervenes:

> This century, with a loss of millions of lives, has underlined the fact that democracy survives as long as it is fought for. It is challenged today across the Atlantic. It is for us, living in the home of parliamentary democracy to decide how we respond to their challenge here in Britain.

We cannot ignore the alarmist aspect of Wilson's speeches. There was no threat to democracy in Britain, however serious the problem. And the parallel with America was as baseless as it was vulgar. It was typical Wilsonian cynicism — a dramatic presentation of the problem to conceal a complete lack of creative social policy.

The black community in Brixton experienced two aspects of state reaction to the youth revolt. Firstly the stick. Panther members were harassed by the Brixton police at every turn. They were picked up as they sold their literature and distributed leaflets. Their headquarters and fundraising functions were raided. They were arrested and charged indiscriminately as they pursued their campaigns. On the eve of the Conference on the Rights of Black People, Special Branch officers raided the headquarters, in Brixton, and rifled the organisation's files. For months on end the Panthers were bogged down in court cases involving their members and supporters. And this repression was repeated throughout those areas where local groups were firmly established.

This period of repression generated the most debilitating consequences. Membership dwindled, and new recruits were hard to come by. Enthusiastic support mellowed into passive sympathy. After all, only the most finely honed ideological maturity could withstand such an onslaught, and the Panthers were not quite there.

Then came the carrot. The government had unfurled their Urban Aid Programme in 1968 — at first without much impact. Slowly, they filtered small sums of money into the black community, aimed, they said, at ameliorating the problems of young blacks. The programme was conceived in the Home Office Children's Department and its major thrust was the social control of young blacks in revolt. The funds cascaded, eventually, under the Inner City Partnership and the Community Relations Self–Help programme. Millions of pounds have been poured into the black communities. By 1973, these radical Black Power organisations, now considerably weakened by the state repression, crumbled before this onslaught of government funds. Young cadres, once headed for the Panthers, now gathered around government financed projects. Organisations, which were once autonomous and politically vibrant, were now transformed into welfare agencies which extended the crippling welfare state into every area of the black existence.

The Panthers and much else besides fell into decline. But their impact on Brixton was enormous. For five years Brixton had experienced an intense, radical politics. Young blacks were introduced, for the first rime, to advanced political organisation and ideas. The militant and organised opposition to the police had percolated down to the very base of the community from which the original inspiration had come. The links had been made nationally, and international concerns were tied into local preoccupations. Then there were those who could link this radical upsurge to its foundations in the anti–colonial movement which dominated Caribbean politics in the pre and post Second World War period. The Panthers had left their mark on Brixton. The community would never be the same again.

The rulers of British society were busily reforming the colonial mould inside which the black population's confinement had to be perpetuated. We were here to labour. Factory managers and their foremen and women saw to it at the work place. The police stood guard in our communities to ensure social obedience, order and discipline. The Irish, the Scots, the Welsh, varied assortments of European immigrants had been processed in this way. It was our turn now.

The Panthers had cracked that mould and replastering was the order of the day in Brixton as it was in Notting Hill, Moss Side, Leeds, and other inner city areas where blacks were residing and reproducing themselves.

First on the agenda was the fortification of police power. The government set about a technological revolution in policing. A wide range of new gadgetry for surveillance and increased mobility was made available to the police. Specially constructed police stations replaced the traditional buildings. Administrative manipulation and case law extended police powers. The Association of Chief Constables, the feudal barons who run Britain's police forces, exercised a power and authority in relation to governments which bordered on the unconstitutional. Locked in committees behind closed doors in Whitehall, this body demanded and got from government literally what it wanted. Its power owed much to the fact that successive governments, lacking in policy in regard to the escalation of unemployment among young blacks, relied exclusively on the police to contain this section of the population which increased in numbers by the day.

It is no exaggeration to note that thousands and thousands of young blacks have grown up in British society having little contact with any other section of British society but the police and courts. They have developed in the shadow of the SPG, the Vice Squad, the Flying Squad, the Starskys and Hutches of the panda car brigade, the Old Bailey, Inner London Sessions etc. These young blacks spend a major portion of their day contemplating, plotting, planning and scheming against the advance of police power and judicial extremities.

And it is police power devoid of the traditional constraints. By and large the traditional vigilance through which democratic Britain had contained police power and indiscipline was exchanged for free licence. An economic recession was at hand, the blacks were stirring and the Irish had given an indication of how tensions in the United Kingdom would develop. Fearful of the impending revolt and lacking in a social and political policy, which would involve young blacks in the development of British society, successive governments gave full reign to the coercive powers. The police proceeded, with their confidence growing by the day, to trample wildly over the rights of the black community; all this behind the backs of society at large. Judges and magistrates provided uncritical support for the most unorthodox of police methods.

This unrestrained licence which the police enjoyed had disastrous consequences within the force itself. The technological revolution undermined all internal structures; the ensuing lack of control plunged the police into the most damnable corruption. Take note of these statistics: between 1969 and 1972 a score of London detectives went to gaol and hundreds more left the force in disgrace. Even the most conservative fanatic could not deny that this was the tip of the iceberg. An entire elite drug squad appeared in the dock at the Old Bailey when a drug ring comprising police officers of the Drug Squad and black drug dealers was exposed. Most of the black dealers were Brixton based. Not a month passes without some investigation into any one of the police forces in the country. In 1980 close to seven such investigations were proceeding at the same time. And the most damnable corruption of all triggered Operation Countryman which sought to investigate the complicity of police officers in bank robbery, extortion and murder.

That story needs to be told. Operation Countryman was set up in late 1978 to conduct a wide ranging investigation into Scotland Yard and the CID throughout London. The officers who staffed the Countryman team were recruited from West Country police forces. These officers were obstructed at every tum by the senior police officers in London, the Home Office and the Department of Public Prosecutions. The operation revealed corruption of a serious nature at the highest echelons of the police force, up to the level of Assistant Commissioner. The government panicked at the prospect of a mass revelation of the facts and wound down the investigation after spending £3,000,000 on it. Only a handful of junior officers have been prosecuted. All this in full view of the black population. Revelations of police corruption did not serve to educate the black community, simply to confirm that what they were experiencing had spread like a cancer, poisoning relations between the police and other sections of society.

A refurbished public relations department, based at Scotland Yard, came to public view in 1968. They juggled with statistics, manipulated the press, were allowed unlimited access to the media in a consistent slander on the black community. They cosseted every chauvinistic instinct in the indigenous population, gave voice to every meaningless scheme concocted by the cynics who run police forces throughout the country, elevated, to dramatic proportions, the slightest injury suffered by a police officer in the execution of his duty. They trotted out the wives, the children and the mothers to brighten up the facade. Behind all this graft, corruption and illegality prevailed.

And for 10 years there has been little overt, consistent, political opposition coming from the black community. It has been a veritable desert with only the odd moments of political offensive. And what is the cause? We need a thorough examination here.

Side by side with the increase of police power ran the

development of black compromise. Out of the ashes of the Panthers, there emerged the proliferation of a whole host of state financed projects. In Brixton the dying organisation of Jamaican nationals, which had declined along with the practice of ushering defendants to solicitors and formulating complaints to Scotland Yard and Members of Parliament, received a new lease of life. A strong injection of government funds transformed this carcass into the Brixton Neighbourhood Centre, which reinstituted the old approach. Staffed by blacks, they would repeat the worn out formulae of yesteryear. The higgledy–piggledy arrangement, which was the Railton Youth Club, was thrown at once into the vanguard of modernity. The Melting Pot Foundation struck gold and launched into youth hostels, a mystification for the ghettoisation of young blacks. Later, Sabarr Books staked its claim to a small fortune. The Abeng Centre, the Black Ink Collective, the Black Women's Group, the Brixton Law Centre and the local Community Relations Council appeared as the outer layer of the replastered colonial mould.

And who are these folk who have been drawn into sustaining colonial social relations here in Brixton? Firstly, there are those who perceive themselves as a cut above the ordinary labourer. Failed businessmen and women of the older generation, they have sought social elevation by way of government grants. They are immersed in venality and ruthless in their fraudulent acquisition of government funds for personal use. What is important here is not the moral issue. It is that the police, the government and those agencies, who parcel out government funds, are fully aware of these types and what they do. But official society needs them and is willing to use them.

Then there are the born again blacks who are distinguishable from the mass of blacks by educational attainment. And here I refer to those who are unable to take five GCE '0' levels in their stride. Among them, a university degree conjures up expectations of the most grandiose kind. Meritocrats they all are. Plunged into the fiercely competitive world of the meritocracy, they cry racial discrimination at the slightest opportunity in order to cover up their individual inadequacies. They have retreated into the world of black projects, a terrain which they guard ferociously at the slightest sign of white encroachment. They sound radical enough, but on close inspection their hostility to the white working class disguises an even greater hostility to its black counterpart.

For the past 10 years, here in Brixton, they have abjured all political campaigns, all militant stances on the police question. And finally the political entryists. These projects, they hope, will provide access to rebellious blacks from which they would attempt the recruitment of members for the Labour Party, the Communist Party, the International Marxist Group, the Socialist Workers Party et al.

It is from this milieu that the police have managed to draw assistance for a propaganda coup which has succeeded in pulling the wool over the eyes of sections of the host society for 10 years. The name of the game has been the police liaison committee. Gathered in this empty shell are police officers and representatives of projects, there to discuss relations between blacks and the police with regard to the improvement of such relations.

It is the most vulgar whitewash. The police representatives are not representing the police and the black representatives are not representing the black community. It is merely a cloak to cover up the continuing escalation of the struggle between the police and the black community. What amazes is the fact that official society staked all and continues so to do on this meaningless exercise.

By the mid 1970s the new social arrangement had been established. Policing had been revolutionised, police power had been afforded free licence and a section of the black community emerged from the ashes of the Panthers to give some impression that something positive was at hand. They proceeded to the eighties arm in arm with the police on their liaison committees. Those who stayed away from these committees kept within those limits which ensured that next year's grant was safe.

The replastered mould, the new social arrangement, meant that there was little possibility of a Joshua Francis campaign recurring. From the mid seventies and after, those who suffered experiences similar to Joshua Francis went to the Law Centre, the Brixton Neighbourhood Centre, Railton Youth Club, the Abeng or St Matthews. No campaign resulted, militancy was out of the question. Where previously the Panthers linked Francis' case with Campbell's, with Bro Tex and others, the projects kept each case in its little cubicle. Each experience was atomised never to jell into an organic and vibrant organisational movement. This atomisation led to a 10 year period of organisational paralysis.

Meanwhile, several profound changes were taking place within the mould itself. The sharpening of the economic recession increased the numbers of young blacks who could not find jobs. Their presence on the streets heightened the conflict between them and the police. The very existence of these various projects teased the black community into expectations which delivered no change whatever, with the result that the most intense passions were being concentrated inside the mould itself. From time to time those passions exploded into open violence. Who better to articulate these moments than the police themselves? In a memorandum to the Select Committee on Race Relations and Immigration, March 1976, Scotland Yard made the following admission:

> Recently there has been a growth in the tendency for members of London's West Indian communities to combine against police by interfering with police officers who are effecting the arrest of a black person or who are in some way enforcing the law in situations which involve black people. In the last 12 months 40 such incidents have been recorded. Each carries a potential for large–scale disorder. . . Experience indicates that they are more likely to occur during the summer months and that the conflict invariably is with

young West Indians. They can occur anywhere in the Metropolitan Police district, but are of course more likely in those areas which have a high proportion of West Indian settlers.

The historical moment could not have been more clearly described. The demise of the Panthers meant that the black community in Brixton had been deprived of and outmanoeuvred out of an organisational framework through which they could express their revolt politically, through which they could link their experiences with others nationally and internationally. This did not mean revolt was at an end. Revolt was alive and kicking and living in Brixton.

On the evening of 19 June, 1973, young blacks clashed with police at the Brockwell Park fair. Bottles, stones, just about any available missile was thrown at the police. The police called for reinforcements and so did young blacks. The battle raged for half an hour. In those circumstances the police grab and arrest who is at hand. Whether you were fighting or not is irrelevant. Robin Sterling, a young student at Tulse Hill Comprehensive School, once a nursery for the Black Panther Movement, was arrested. He was innocent of the charge of assault on police, so too were Horace Parkinson and Lloyd James. At the end of the day, all three were sent to prison.

Tulse Hill Comprehensive School had retained, in a small organisation, the Brixton Collective, the Panther tradition. They raised a campaign for the freedom of Robin Sterling under the slogans 'Move as a Community' and 'School Today, Jail Tomorrow'. Robin was eventually freed on appeal, not before the Brockwell Three Defence Committee, the creation of the Brixton Collective, had staged a successful strike of school students and a massive demonstration in the South London area.

Within weeks there followed violent clashes between young blacks and the SPG at the Railton Youth Club. Hand to hand fighting ensued. Then, in September 1974, young blacks again took on the police at the Swan disco. One month later the exact scene reproduced itself at Stockwell tube station. Again in June 1976, close to 100 blacks spontaneously marched on Brixton police station following the wrongful arrest of a middle–aged West Indian on Railton Road.

The British government had one solitary reply to this phenomenon which reproduced itself in several black communities up and down the country. Clashes would be followed by intensive police investigations. Such investigations involved the wringing of confessions and statements from participants. Case papers would be sent to the Director of Public Prosecutions who returned charges of Riot and Affray.

From Notting Hill to Wood Green, from Leeds to Bristol, the formula was the same.

The projects sat on case after case ushering young blacks through a maze of judicial procedure, their friends, parents and relatives providing a passive audience for the performing circus of lawyers. This has been the dominant tendency in the black community for the last decade. Young blacks would fight with great courage and when called to order by the state through its courts, the projects relegated them to the back seat and placed the radical lawyer at the helm.

The confidence and social growth which an involvement in political campaigns brings were denied young blacks and their parents, introducing young blacks, particularly to the violence of despair. Wherever the opposite tendency prevailed (and this was on rare occasions) it has been remarkably successful. The campaign to free North London student Cliff McDaniel, in 1975, led to the formation of the Black Parent's Movement and the Black Student's Movement. The campaign to free George Lindo established strong foundations among the West Indian community in Bradford. Similar campaigns in Leeds and Manchester generated like successes.

Not until the New Cross Fire, which claimed the lives of 13 young blacks, was political campaigning returned to the position of centrality which it occupied in the days of the Panthers and other similar groupings. The gusto and enthusiasm with which the black community gathered in their thousands, on the Black People's Day of Action on 2 March, 1981, indicated the extent to which they had been frustrated by the projects from expressing themselves politically. They were free at last. The mould had once more been shattered. Black Brixtonians walked the streets of Brixton with the confidence that a new era was at hand. They were prepared for Operation Swamp 81*.

*Operation Swamp 81 was mounted by the 'L' (Lambeth) District of the Metropolitan Police, 6 April — 11 April. There were 10 squads, (four assigned to Brixton), of between five and 11 officers in plain clothes in each squad, operating under the following written instructions:

> "The purpose of this Operation is to flood identified areas on 'L' District to detect and arrest burglars and robbers. The essence of the exercise is therefore to ensure that all officers remain on the streets and success will depend on a concentrated effort of 'stops', based on powers of surveillance and suspicion proceeded by persistent and astute questioning."

Brixton 12 April 1981, Sunday afternoon. The confrontation begins on the corner of Coldharbour Lane and Atlantic Road. *Photo: John Sturrock.*

Scarman:
Failing to Grasp the Nettle

Whatever else Lord Scarman had to do, there were two major tasks before him. First, his report had to show that he grasped the essence of the historical moment in its entirety. The British people needed to be informed of those essential characteristics which distinguished the summer uprisings from anything that had gone before. Only by extracting these characteristics would Lord Scarman have been able to fashion the foundations of his report from which his recommendations would automatically flow; recommendations which would reflect and harmonise with the range and depth of the revolt.

Secondly, he had to recommend not what is possible for a Tory government led by Mrs Thatcher to accept; not what police officers may or may not be happy with, but what is historically required to restore the balance of power which had, over a quarter of a century, leaned heavily in favour of the police.

Yet again, official society has failed to grasp the nettle. The Scarman report is way off beam in all matters that are essential and crucial. I aim to prove and to give others the opportunity of proving it for themselves.

Three central features emerge out of the revolts on which any report must rest. First, within 10 minutes of the Brixton uprising, a body of about 30 young men gathered and began to transform a spontaneous reaction into an organised revolt. They coolly set in motion and supervised the mounting of barricades and the manufacture of petrol bombs. They organised scouts, who moved around on roller skates and bicycles, returning with detailed information on enemy positions.

They organised the commandeering of vehicles, set in train diversionary actions to confuse the enemy. They selected which buildings would be destroyed by fire and saw to it that they were. They organised points where those who were injured were attended, all the while in touch with developments within the area affected by the revolt. Finally, they took a decision to retreat, which the mass of young blacks promptly obeyed.

Such a body of men and women exists in every black community in this country. That is what the revolts reveal. The point was not lost on the Chief Constable of Manchester. Describing his experience on the streets of Moss Side he said: "I have described it already as a form of guerrilla warfare and that's precisely what it is. They (young blacks) employed unique and extraordinary tactics and last night we had to be extremely flexible in our nature and ability to respond."

Secondly, West Indian parents are not prepared to make or to throw petrol bombs at the police. I have discovered, though, that once young blacks act in this way, older West Indians are prepared to offer them sympathy and support. This represents a profound transformation in attitudes.

Thirdly, we in the West Indian community have refrained in the past from taking drastic action, fearing the much touted white backlash. It has not come, and there is little possibility that it will. Something else has happened. Young whites joined the revolt.

This brings me to the crucial question. Why is it that the best elements in official society are unable to grasp the nettle? And by best elements I mean those who are not prepared to respond, at this stage, with extreme and brutal blood shedding. How could Lord Scarman ignore such significant developments? The answer lies in one word, myth. They are constrained, inhibited and dominated by the myth that the British police are the best in the world.

The British people, in the course of neutralising a powerful monarchy, established parliamentary democracy and in the process developed a sense of democracy and freedom over and beyond that existing in most other countries. Later, millions of ordinary working people combined to add greater weight and depth to the democratic tradition. It is this developed instinct for democracy and freedom which has kept the British police in check, which has ensured that restraints on the police be written into law. In addition, the British people have, for centuries, practised an alertness and vigilance which ensured that any attempt by the police to break out of the legal and administrative constraints was powerfully resisted. Once these constraints are absent, it has been proved that the British police are capable of all the excesses which characterise other police forces.

That has been the West Indian community's experience. For some considerable time we lacked the alertness and vigilance which a vibrant community produces. The police sensed this and trampled wildly on blacks' rights. An extensive body of experience exists to support these allegations.

To this formidable police power, successive governments, over the last 10 years, have added exceptional powers of stop and search. I am prepared to accept that parliamentarians, in giving these powers to the police, thought the police would exercise them discreetly.

But a police force with a capacity for discreetly employing stop and search powers in the black community had long ceased to exist, except in the parliamentarians' minds. The British police have used these powers to express every whim, caprice and prejudice imaginable. And it is in this context that Operation Swamp was formulated.

There was only one force in British society capable of bringing Operation Swamp to an end, and that was the black community in revolt. That was and is the last card, and in playing it the black community laid the basis for an equitable reconstruction.

Lord Scarman's recommendations and their implementation needed to create a political impact comparable to that which their revolt had generated. Liaison, community policing, an independent element in complaints and his vacillation on accountability remain peripheral unless accompanied by a radical and central thrust capable of correcting the gross, historical imbalance. His entire package has failed to meet this vital requirement. It is mere tinkering.

He had the opportunity to demand the immediate abolition of all powers of stop and search. Not at some future uncertain date but now. Twenty-five years of history demanded that stringent safeguards aimed at protecting the suspect from physical abuse, verbals and forced confessions be enacted at once. And finally, the experiences of the West Indian community at the hands of magistrates screamed for the recommendation that the Lord Chancellor issue guidelines to magistrates requiring the highest standards of police evidence before defendants are convicted.

Such a package would represent a modest beginning, but it would certainly have meant to the West Indian community that at last a government was willing to tackle this problem in a fundamental way. Lord Scarman's failure to act along these lines has ensured that those forms which appeared in embryo on the streets of Britain's cities must necessarily develop into full-blown manifestations in the not too distant future.

Notting Hill Carnival 1978. *Photo: John Sturrock*

Revolt of the Underclass

In the heart of Brixton, just off Railton Road where the April uprising began, are to be found the offices of Race Today. Its editor is Darcus Howe, a 38-year-old Trinidadian. Howe is one of the best known black activists in Britain, and three weeks ago we *[Village Voice]* talked with him at length: about the uprisings, about developments in the Afro-Caribbean and Asian communities, and about his perspective of political options, both for blacks and whites. His views were often far from predictable.

Darcus Howe: We were persuaded, encouraged to come to Britain, to be hewers of wood and drawers of water. The perception of this new section of working people went as follows: we would rigidly concern ourselves with work; we would have no leisure; we would, without deviation, get there in the morning, come home in the evening, go to bed, go back there in the morning, come home in the afternoon, go to bed. Any relaxation of that discipline would undermine the exclusive reason for why we were here. So when West Indians held parties in their homes to ease the tensions of the working day, the police would raid them, to suppress them. Any form of leisure activity at all that we were involved in, anything other than on the way to and from work, we were harassed. So if you were unemployed and weren't working and you were found around the streets of London, there was a charge which they resurrected called 'sus', 'being a suspicious person', a charge going back centuries, when they sought to curb the unemployed in the early period of British industrialisation.

It is necessary to identify these reasons because we tend to get carried away by this exclusive question of race, without taking into consideration the fundamental reasons. Of course race is used to justify it, once it takes place. It gives it an extra impetus, but it is not fundamental. That's the first point.

The second point is this: we have come up against — in posing the question of the behaviour of the British police — a formidable hurdle. I describe it in this way: it's a myth, all the more powerful because it contains elements of truth, that the British police are the best in the world. It is truth turned on its head. What is the case is that the mass of the British population, having neutralised a very powerful monarchy and having established parliamentary democracy, developed — I believe — a very strong democratic instinct and a very strong sense of freedom that ensured that the British police were hemmed in by a set of rules and regulations. But whenever those constraints are absent, the British police are capable of all the excesses which can be perpetrated by modern police forces. All.

And the Caribbean peoples, who are always reminded of slavery at the slightest hint of oppression, have revolted in a way that no one has seen in Britain in the last hundred years. It is an historical moment of extreme significance, not only for ourselves but for society as a whole.

Why did this historical moment occur in 1981?

Several factors. The major one is a change in the composition of the black community. Those of us who came here in the late '50s and early '60s were constrained by the myth that we were going home sooner or later, that we would earn some money and go, and therefore tended to put up with things that we knew were wrong and discussed with each other as being illegal and against any conception of human rights. But there are young blacks who were born here, who have grown up here, who eat bangers and mash, egg and chips, with the same ease as their white counterparts, who sat in the same classrooms with them, who knew that they weren't in any way superior to them, and once the police encountered that generation, they met with a completely different attitude.

Because the older West Indian population had been separated socially from their white counterparts–they didn't mix – they had no measure of what whites thought. All assessment of your white fellow workers was governed by myth and prejudice. But the younger ones went to school with those kids. One of the myths that constrained us was that there would be a white backlash if we acted. The younger ones know that that isn't so. They know that the young whites have the same problems.

You were born when?
In 1943, in a small fishing village in Trinidad. I removed from there to another small village in which the only thing people did in the main was plant, tend, and reap sugar cane. My father was headmaster of the local Church of England school. My mother taught there. So we lived in the headmaster's house. The church was next door. The graveyard was at the back and the school was in the same compound. So I was part of the village but yet not part of it. There we were — our home a small oasis in a desert of ignorance — and I won a scholarship at the age of 10 to go to a grammar school in Port of Spain. I read the classics, French literature, English literature, a lot of the Latin classics, and Spanish literature.

After leaving school the Caribbean cramped me, like a miasma. Couldn't get out of it. Had to get out. In 1960, 1961. In fact so horrific it was for me that I plunged at once into gang warfare in Trinidad and went to court and to prison. I know now why. I was going crazy. Here in my head were the most advanced, reasoned, philosophical, and cultural artefacts of Europe and

I was living in a proletarian area dominated by ignorance and myth. The contradiction was sharp and I thought, fuck it, I'm going to be a bandit, an extreme criminal. And I almost destroyed myself. If you go back to that urban area in which I spent my teens people will say, Darcus Howe, he was crazy.

I came here, after a lot of trial and tribulation, breaking my parents' hearts. Eighteen, young and hot.

You were active in Black Power.

Oh yes, I was in the Black Power movement and one of the main exponents of it. But there was something which nagged me all the time. You cast out Whitey, but there is a certain integrity in my educational discipline. If you are a creature of reason, you could express emotion from time to time when reason is called for. But unless you degenerate into corruption, you have to get out of it.

So you rejected the Black Power approach...

I won't say rejected. I incorporated the best of it and went my way, I am not about not speaking to white people, or not having them in meetings. I talk to anybody — I feel strong enough.

You feel the organisation of the future has nothing to do with a black political entity and a white political entity.

It can't have. It's like cowboys and Indians. That doesn't mean I compromise an inch on the question of race. It makes me fiercer on the issue of race, because I'm confident about it. I won't have it. It's not on.

There is bad housing, unemployment, and the problems of a bald and demoralising environment but this is not the central issue which moved the bulk of young blacks to insurrection: it is the police. The question that faces us all is whether their powers will be increased, or whether there will be a massive reduction of police power. That is a serious political question and it turns on what moral and political force one can gather at their doors to ensure that police power is reduced.

So, concerning the police, what would you specifically advocate?

There's a new and very dangerous tendency which creeps into all these matters. They now invest the police with political powers. We don't vote for them. We don't elect them, but suddenly we are asked to have discussions with them on social and political questions. I am against that, for this reason: they have a tremendous amount of power and I have none, so it's an unequal discussion.

. . . which institutionalises the inequality.

Absolutely. I will talk to them if a burglar comes into my house. That's when I speak to them. If I want some direction about where a particular street is, I ask a police officer. Those areas in which you speak to the police must be so strictly defined that they won't be able to creep out of that into general discussion.

So what you want are laws to curb the police. It's as simple as that.

Absolutely. The reinstitution of civil power over institutionalised, coercive power. Heavy discipline.

Now in the US we see the weight of the Reaganite attack being felt first and foremost by the poor, notably by blacks and to an extent Hispanics. We see no particularly inspiring black leadership. Given the Thatcherite attack in Great Britain on social spending, what sort of parallels do you see?

I'm not worried about blacks, Hispanics, and Chicanos in the United States, for this reason; they'll come again. I am absolutely sure in my own mind that the period we are going through now in regard to blacks in the United States is a period of downturn and the movement will rise again. It is crucial for us to record that a lot of our political attitudes and organisational formations were influenced by what took place in the United States in the '60s and the '70s. And a lot of mistakes that they made we are able to avoid. Why it is so difficult for them in the United States is that when you emerge, they kill you, and once you emerge organisationally they destroy it with a kind of ruthlessness which is unimaginable.

But there is an essential difference which must always be pointed out. You can walk through Harlem all night and not see a white face, except passing in a car. You walk in parts of Florida, Miami, and not see a white face. But that's not the case in Britain. We are socialised with whites. We see them every day. We move with them every day. So it is difficult for them to carry out that kind of repression on us in isolation. If they could, they would, you know. But they can't. And they cannot guarantee what whites would do, because whites were revolting with young blacks in the insurrections. Young whites.

So what is going on, socially and politically, in terms of black organisation?

The riots opened up an entirely new political ethos. To understand the organisational stages that we are moving to, it is essential to know that in the late 1960s there were Black Power organisations in almost every city in this country. A combination of repression — not as sharp as in the United States — but repression British style and Harold Wilson's political cynicism undermined that movement. What he did was to offer a lot of money to the black community, which set up all kinds of advice centres and projects for this and projects for that. So, in some black communities, if you have a headache somebody is on to you saying, 'Well, look, I have a project for blacks with headaches.' That paralysed the political initiative of blacks. It was done for you by the state and, as you know, Britain is saturated with the concept of welfare. The riots have broken through that completely, smashed it to smithereens, indicating that it was no palliative, no cure for the cancer.

So, after welfarism, what is the new ethos?
The best example of it, without speculating but taking what exists now, is this: on 18 January, 1981, in New Cross, London, 13 young blacks were killed in a fire, mysteriously. Because of increasing racial attacks against blacks by a fringe of whites since 1976, the entire black community suspected that those kids were firebombed. They were fire–bombed at a house party by white racists. That happened on a Sunday morning.

That Sunday evening, some of us decided we would call a meeting a week later, a public meeting, and we needed on the Tuesday before the public meeting to have a group of organisations come. Our most hopeful expectations were for 20 people. Four hundred people turned up from all over the country. Only West Indians. And there a new institution was formed, the Black Assembly, which met week after week until 2 March, and called a demonstration, the Black People's Day of Action. Fifteen thousand people turned up, and it was the first instance of mass mobilisation, that mass mobilisation which had been choked and clogged up inside the womb of the black community over a period of 10 years with all these projects.

You are looking toward a black/white mass organisation?
Black/white mass movement. But one always must point to what we are heading for. What are we aiming for? Are we aiming for the vulgarity of a better standard of living. I think a passion has arisen in the breasts of millions of people in the world for a kind of democratic form and shape which would transcend parliamentary democracy in its creativity and innovation.

One who lives in the United States cannot but be aware of the structural, endemic racism. In Britain today, do you see racism as diminishing or increasing? How much of a factor is it in political organisation?
There is a double–edgedness to what you have said about the United States. When blacks tell me that, I understand it, but I smile inwardly, because a lot that they do they have learned

from and with whites, white workers, in the way in which they organise themselves, the way in which they organized the CIO, and a lot of blacks came into it. So on the one hand you see racists but on the other hand you employ a lot of the means of revolt that whites have used. So I take the racist point, but I take another point as well: the definition of politics. You have to be able to transform that tendency into the dominant tendency, and it needs a lot of political skill and a lot of faith to do it. You have to see them lynching you and know something else. Otherwise you never transcend the hurdle. You accept the prevailing ethos. That is what distinguishes a radical from a revolutionary. The radical is trapped by the prevailing barriers — and they are enormous in the United States. Maybe I say that with the luxury of living in Britain.

Okay, let's look at racism in Britain. It is presumably found in the competition for jobs, in union situations, quite apart from the experiences of everyday life.
The competition for jobs leads two ways. In meeting each other in the competition, we either decide not to compete anymore or we take that competition to its logical conclusion. What prevents you from taking competition to the logical conclusion is that Britain has a sense of class. The working class has a sense of itself, and when you go to America you know how important that is. Working people in Britain tend to see being working class as a virtue.

So class is dominant over race in Britain?
Dominant. It could cease being so, you know. One has to fight to keep it that way.

But let's look at a likely future for Britain: enormous structural unemployment, the creation of a permanent underclass...
Permanent unemployment, that is what is on the agenda, with the revolutionising of production with the microchip. Now what

the British working class has to do is to break out of this demand for jobs, which characterised the 1930s, the Jarrow marches, and so on. They will have to lift themselves to this new reality, which will of course call for the merciless shortening of the working day, the working week, and the working life, and a concentration on the debate that is going on — and that is the debate missed by a lot of the old-style trade unionists and the old-style institutions like the trade union bureaucracy and the Labour Party.

I look at young blacks. If you look at the development of Rastafarianism on such a massive scale, this cannot be separated in my view from the material basis and growing consciousness that one will not work again and one must now be concerned with what is life? Is there a God? Who is he? What is the relationship between yourself and your kind? That is the creeping development of Rastafarianism.

The first set of people to know that there ain't no work anymore were ex-slaves. From the moment we came off the plantation, labour-intensive, and you started to present us with factories, there was no work ever again. That is new to the advanced countries, but to the under-developed countries it has always been so. I could take you to Port of Spain now and point to him, him, and him and say he is a grandfather and he never worked in his life. This is a grandmother who never worked in her life. We come easy to it. But here, they say, 'March for Jobs'. What jobs?

It's stimulating to hear you say this, because the left seems to have a lot of illusions about this. The slogan should really be, 'Less Work', not 'More Work'.
'Less work, more money'. And that's a vulgarity too. 'Less work, more leisure'. We have built up over the centuries the techno-logical capacity to release people from that kind of servitude.

So then you have to talk about redistribution of wealth.
Redistribution. A completely new ethos. And we are on the verge of it.

Don't you think that pathological symptoms, including racism, will increase as people fight on the scrap heap, as the economy goes down?

I agree. Something else increases too. Side by side, living in the same atom with pathology, is the possibility to leap. So the oppositions are a client populace, battling for a little bit more of a slice. Crabs in a barrel. Or you leap. The leap depends among other things on what dominant political ideology is presented to the population.

You view the current decline of the Labour Party with considerable optimism?

Considerable optimism. The Labour Party is a creature of a certain moment in the material organisation of society, and the forces which arise from this. It's work, it's welfare. It's getting some things to the ordinary working people, which of course I understand. When you read, especially in the novels, I think there you get much more penetrating insights into life and society than those offered by politicians. The poverty of the mining population when people would have to wrap cloth around their feet to keep warm — that doesn't exist in Britain anymore. Nor will people permit it. Either they are driven back to that, or something else happens. My view is that the Labour Party is an instrument that was necessary for that period.

What about the white fascist organisations in Britain and their rise?

They have grown here. They developed, but they have lost every single election, they have lost their deposits. They kill people. There was a man recently who decided for his twenty-first birthday to kill 10 blacks. But why should I elevate that to something of tremendous proportions? In the First World War they killed 10 million, in the Second, they killed more. Stalin liquidated so many people in the USSR. So you kill as you can. If one guy wants to kill ten then he is part of the barbarism. They killed 10 million and they get elevated to the House of Lords.

Biographies are written in their name. They killed 10 million people. I find that astonishing. So if a young man decides to kill 10, that's just killing.

But if many young men decide to get together in a movement...
We feel strong enough to really get back at their backsides. Are they a significant force? No. They are just the dregs of a civilisation. Nothing significant. I wouldn't elevate it, though I am on guard against it. You see these windows (which have grilles on them), I have to take my guard. But the mass of white British people are against them. . .

It was six in the evening and outside the *Race Today* offices people were sloshing through the puddles on the way home from work, or standing about in doorways. Howe got up and stretched, then picked up a document.
"Listen to this," he said. "After the uprising in Moss Side last July they appointed a local Manchester barrister called Hynter to enquire into what happened, and how it started. Here's what he writes:

> 'At about 10.20pm a responsible and in our view reliable mature black citizen was in Moss Lane East, and observed a large number of black youths whom he recognised as having come from a club a mile away. At the same time a horde of white youths came up the road from the direction of Moss Side. He spoke to them and ascertained they were from Withenshawe. The two groups met and joined. There was nothing in the manner of their meeting which in any way reflected a pre-arranged plan. There was a sudden shout and the mob stormed off in the direction of Moss Side police station. We are given an account by another witness who saw the mob approach the station, led, so it was claimed, by a nine-year-old boy with those with Liverpool accents in the van.'

Howe smiled: "Whites from Withenshawe, blacks from Moss Side, no pre-arranged plan. They gather. There is a shout, 'On to Moss Side police station'. That gives you some indication. You must have a convergence of interests in order for that to happen."

Darcus Howe during the protests over the New Cross fire, 1981.
Photo: Socialist Worker Archive

The Shoe That Didn't Pinch

On Thursday last week, I went to the West End to purchase a pair of shoes. I left the offices of Race Today, the journal I edit, shortly after 4pm. We are based in Brixton.

Michael Cadette, a fellow member of the Race Today Collective, accompanied me. He is young, mildly trendy, and knows more than I do of men's clothing. He recommended Succhi's on the corner of Regent Street and Oxford Street, Bertie's, and Woodhouse, both further west along Oxford Street, with the convincing rider that, at all three shops, bargain sales offered quality shoes at reduced prices.

We made our way by underground to Oxford Circus. Out of the station and we are right on top of the Succhi shop. We enter, browse around and target a pair. Should we draw a blank at Bertie's and Woodhouse, we would return.

We walk briskly along Oxford Street. We know our destination and there is no need to hesitate.

Ten yards away from Bertie's we pass two uniformed police officers, both quite young. We nip into Bertie's and Michael introduces me to the shop assistant who is his ex–girlfriend's sister. We inquire about a particular range and are told that it has been sold out. We go next door to Woodhouse, survey the display and are not moved to purchase. We decide, spontaneously, to head for the Bally shoe shop. We are now on the pavement immediately outside Woodhouse when two uniformed police officers approach us. I recognise them as the two officers we passed earlier. PC C411 directed his questions to me.

"I want to ask you some questions," he teased.

"Certainly," I replied.

"What is your name?" he asked tentatively.

"Darcus Howe," I replied.

"Where do you live?"

"Brixton," short and sharp.

He seemed less self-assured now, a little nervous.

"I have been observing you along Oxford Street," he said hesitantly, "and you have been acting suspiciously."

"Officer," I inquired sharply, "have you taken leave of your senses? Are you crazy?"

"No, I am not crazy." He was sweating now.

"I saw you and your mate attempt to steal from women's handbags along Oxford Street."

"You saw nothing of the sort. You are a liar and a cheat," I bellowed.

A small crowd gathered. He hummed and hawed for a bit.

"I am going to search you." Now beads of perspiration poured from beneath his helmet.

"Search me, s-e-a-r-chh me," I stumbled.

"You will do nothing of the sort. Go to hell," I rejoined.

Struggling to regain his composure, he warned,

"This is your last chance. Are you going to allow me to search you?"

"Go to hell," I repeated, perhaps somewhat fiercely.

"You will do no such thing." His authority flagged miserably.

"You are under arrest under Section 68, no, Section 66 of the Metropolitan Police Act 1839," he muttered.

"Fine," I replied.

C411 turned his attention to Cadette. He threatened Michael that he would be arrested if he refused to be searched. Michael complied.

Eventually, the van arrived, some 20 minutes after the call. Those 20 minutes were not exactly without moments of torrid invective.

We alight at West End Central police station and are taken into the detention room. Michael is placed in the far corner and I am close to the door. PC C411 draws up a chair on the other side of the table which separates us. He takes my name and address on an official form and leaves the room. He returns after three minutes with a sergeant who sits in the chair just now occupied by C411. He stands awkwardly to the sergeant's left.

I am asked to empty my pockets, which I do. The sergeant dutifully itemises my property on a massive form. That bureaucratic task is at an end when he asks C411 what was I arrested for.

Pay close attention. I aim to capture the moment as precisely as I can. C411 fixed his eyes on a sheet of paper lying on the desk. He would not look away from his focus for the next minute. He babbled, spluttered and squirmed: "I was walking along Oxford Street with Police Cadet Willis when I noticed three men in front of me. The third man was wearing a blue windcheater with a red stripe. These two men, Howe and Cadette, entered six shops while the third man stood outside, Police Cadet Willis and myself approached the third man who immediately ran off. We did not chase him because the street was crowded. Both these men came out of the shop looking for the third man and I detained them. They refused to be searched and I arrested them."

Not a word about women's handbags. The sergeant would give nothing away. "What have you got to say, Mr Howe, about what the officer has just said?" he asked matter of factly.

'The officer is crazy," I offered.

The sergeant turned the sheet on which I had signed that my belongings were properly recorded and invited me to sign the receipt form.

"But I have only this minute signed in my property," I mused aloud. "Mr Howe, sign the receipt and be on your way." The sergeant was firm and conclusive. I signed and left. Michael joined me 10 minutes later. I bought my shoes eventually, and a neck tie as a bonus. I am placing this account, verbatim, before the Home Secretary and the Commissioner of Police with the covering note as follows: "Dear Sir, I enclose documentation of my experiences with two of your police officers. Do what you will."

Police retreat under a hail of bricks and bottles Notting Hill Carnival 1976.
Photo: Socialist Worker Archive

'Is A Police Carnival'
Darcus Howe
September 1976

Darcus Howe, editor of *Race Today,* **has participated in Carnival since its inception. We asked him to write a personal diary of his experiences and observations at Carnival this year, and below, we publish his account.**

This was my eleventh Carnival. I have been participating in it since its inception in 1965, sometimes as a reveller and sometimes at various levels in the organisation of the event. Once it emerged in January 1976 that police, local councillors and a few white residents were determined to have the Carnival removed from the streets of Notting Hill, the *Race Today* Collective asked me to carry out a campaign in our journal, aimed at winning the struggle to retain the festival on the streets. In the February, April and May issues of *Race Today*, we sought to demolish the frivolous objections of the opposition and we outlined what we felt to be the responsibility of the organisers of Carnival.

The opposition mobilised a petition and Chief Superintendent Patterson received it, posing, petition held high, for photographs in the local press. In his capacity as the senior police officer responsible for the Notting Hill area, he exploited the local press to the full, as well as trying to split the organising committee, threatening, cajoling and manoeuvring. Mrs Lennon, spokeswoman for the white residents, threatened a High Court injunction if she did not have her way. Alderman Methuen, deputy leader of the local council, sought the support of the Home Secretary.

Patterson, we are told, waved a copy of *Race Today* before the Carnival organisers protesting the contents. To all our accusations about his activities and manoeuvrings, we received no reply. The same cannot be said for Methuen. He wrote to *Race Today* complaining about the tone of our article and our editorial policy. We published these. The chairman of the Carnival Committee visited our offices. We outlined our strategy and won his cooperation. It was a hard–fought campaign, and by 3 April, we were the victors. It was Carnival as usual. Or was it?

The minicab turns into Pembridge Road. We are on our way to the Carnival. Along Pembridge Road, into Chepstow and left into Westbourne Park, there are policemen everywhere. This is Sunday. The minicab stops at the corner of Great Western and Westbourne Park and I make my way towards the Mangrove Restaurant.

The Mangrove is my permanent link with Notting Hill. The streets around link the terrain on which I received my first baptism in the realities of political life. I am on the alert. It is a discipline which most West Indians have learnt when in the presence of police officers. Rhythm and steel penetrate the air. I turn into Powis Terrace and I hear the Ebony Steel band jamming a Kitchener calypso. I meet Pepe, Joe and those brothers and sisters who, for weeks, could talk about nothing else but costumes and sweet–pan. Someone passes me a bottle of vodka and I oblige. I cease counting at twenty uniformed policemen. The jamming continues, then there is a sharp interruption. 'Move on! Move on!', snaps the senior police officer. 'Get moving, get moving.' I cross Westbourne Park and into All Saints Road. I am greeted by the Mangrove crowd on the corner.

'Oh God, Darcus, it's a police Carnival.'

'Boy, it look like the police have dey own band.' The flippant comments betray a feeling of shock, but Terry confirms what we all know: 'It boun' to have trouble, they take too much rass clart liberty.' The comments are now flying thick and fast as we settle down in front of the Mangrove: 'Who it is negotiate wid the police?" Darcus, you ent know that the police was coming out in force?' I confess ignorance. 'Why the Committee ent tell we?'

I leave with a companion and head for 'under de bridge'. It is the other focal point of Carnival. I arrive to witness the first confrontation. A group of blacks surround two police officers: 'Whey yuh take him for?' Wha wrong wid selling drink? Yuh ever hear 'bout a Carnival without drink?' 'All yuh dread. Ah know whey all yuh want, you know. Ah know whey all yuh looking for. Yuh go get it.' I inquire and am told that Chief Superintendent Patterson's Pale Ale Brigade is in action. They locate a vendor who is selling it. They stalk their prey and then pounce. The Pale Ale Brigade registers its first success in the military encounter. I have an image of General Patton, no, Superintendent Patterson, receiving on the radio the first report of success in his Pale Ale Campaign. Within minutes, the Brigade has whisked off a second victim. In frustration someone protests that black people are fuckries for allowing the police to get away with it. I disagree but hold my peace. The confrontation will come but it's early days yet.

Walking around, and searching out, the police operation begins to take shape. There are two central points where police are concentrated. One of them on Acklam Road, opposite the teenage disco; the other situated around the corner from the Mangrove. They sit idly in coaches, reading paperbacks, playing cards, or simply chatting to each other. If they are on hand to search for pickpockets, then Robert Mark has to explain how a police officer does that sitting all day in a bus. No. It is a reserve force ready for the confrontation that Scotland Yard has predicted.

I make my way back to the Mangrove. Ebony is turning

into Lancaster Road still chaperoned by forty-odd uniformed policemen. They are definitely not looking for pickpockets; they have come expecting a confrontation. The bands are chaperoned along a defined route, forty policemen to a band. Along that route, vanloads of policemen are strategically placed. At the first sign of trouble, the forty officers form a cordon, a long line across the street. At the other end, reinforcements are called in and the crowd is sandwiched between two lines of police officers. It is a military strategy to defeat a hostile rebellion.

I return to the Mangrove and as the hours pass by the tension mounts. Bay 57, one of the steel bands, is standing in front of the Mangrove entertaining the crowd. Further along the road there is a scuffle. About seventy cc officers are disgorged from the green coaches parked around the corner. They stampede in the direction of the scuffles. I distinctly hear a police officer say to another beside him, 'This is where it starts.'

New Cross fire protest. 'Blood Ah Go Run If Justice No Come' became a key slogan of the protests. *Photo: Socialist Worker Archive*

Race Today **and the Struggle for Racial Justice** Gareth Peirce

When the warriors of revolutionary movements depart, taking
with them their oratory, the power of their personalities and
their tactical genius, can those movements ever be reproduced?
Most recently, the death of Darcus Howe prompted the realisation that the history of the recent past is elusive — the stra-
tegic underpinning of social rebellion is often not recorded or
too fleetingly to be accessible to later generations. Prompted
by Darcus's death to revisit the history of the end of the last
century causes a separate realisation — that the most famous
initiatives of the small number of brilliant activists of whom
he was part had simultaneously given birth to a myriad of less
recognised collaborations. And that an understanding of these
whilst facing the new nightmares of the twenty–first century
can reinforce renewed respect for their universality and an
appreciation of the urgent need that they be sustained.

Two extraordinary political actions are firmly embedded
in the history of twentieth–century British society: the trial of
the Mangrove Nine in 1971 and the march, 20,000 strong, of
black Britons in 1981 from New Cross to Hyde Park in protest
at the hideous deaths of 13 children killed in a likely racist
arson attack but for which police in response were pressuring
surviving children to confess — to having started the fire.

Using the tools it had honed a decade before, in protests at police treatment of the Mangrove, the same collective applied the same determination; that organisation for unprecedented mass action was essential, inspired by the true concept of equal rights and equal demands. Side-by-side with the bereaved parents, ideas were proffered and a formulation of demands evolved, together with the energy and determination to mark indelibly what every part of English society had ignored: 13 dead and nothing said. And beyond the march, when the inquest into the 13 deaths, presided over by a buffoon of a coroner, allowed the mendacious police narrative to be aired, the opportunity for its demolition was as dramatically and publicly seized as a decade before, once the arrests of the Mangrove Nine and the progression of their trial had brought into court, explosively, the collective experience of black citizens in Britain, searingly differently treated, gratuitously beaten, falsely accused and repeatedly framed by the police.

In forceful resistance to the repeated targeting of the Mangrove Restaurant (a lightning rod for police attention as a loved and loving haven for its clientele), it having become a symbol for the exercise of police power, the activists had turned the tables and made it a symbol of black resistance. And when refusal, by forceful protest, to take any more from the state triggered in turn charges of riot, a second radical strategy was mandated within the court, a root-and-branch attack to the entire criminal justice system — the corruption and mendacity and criminality of the police, the bias of the judicial system and the racism of the media.

The exercise of radical refusal by black people to submit themselves to the tyrannies of the state was to become, for others, whether initially conceived of as such or not, an authentic methodology. In this, the same collective group could and did support and guide others — almost all young, most of whom had never heard of the Mangrove trial but who in turn found themselves at the epicentre of conflict and accusation.

The political courage shared with them had been first

triggered but thereafter enriched by the experience of successful rebellion — the concept of collective support and tactical thinking, of taking the accuser on and turning the tables, armed with the confidence to assert that the history of British rights in English law, some forgotten, was there to be reclaimed and used by all, equally, in this country.

On the day, for Bristol youth in 1980, no such intellectual weaponry was to hand when they fought police in pitched battles and drove them out of St Paul's. With no political grounding and no collective organisation, the Bristol uprising, as many others in the years that followed, was triggered by precisely the same combination of brutal, swamping, racist police practices as had demanded the Mangrove resistance in 1970. The spontaneous combustions in St Paul's represented the accumulation of state violence, arbitrary stops and searches and arrests, and the instinctive reaction of new generations who could not tolerate a daily diet of oppression.

The state's reaction? — To charge a dozen arbitrarily selected defendants with riot, the same ancient charge that carried a maximum sentence of life imprisonment. It was tempting for a young person in the dock to refute his claimed identification by police — for throwing stones or smashing the windscreen of an oncoming police car — and say the evidence was mistaken and whoever was involved, it was not him. What took extraordinary courage but was fortified by the experience of the Mangrove defendants, was instead to tell the jury, 'Yes, the police marched into our community to crush us, to harass us, to arrest us, to oppress us, to injure us, to beat us and we had to fight back. This was self-defence, our right.'

And before the jury in Bristol Crown Court was empanelled, their lawyers could insist, just as the Mangrove Nine had a decade before, that the black youths to be put on trial in Bristol Crown Court had a further fundamental right: to a jury of their peers. If the random selection of the jury panel had in fact omitted summonsing jurors from the areas of Bristol in which black citizens predominantly lived, then the selection had to be undertaken again — and was. The history of the experiences of the youth of St Paul's at the hands of police was played out in court, before a representative jury. And the defendants' articulation of their right to self-defence and its acceptance by the jury meant that by the verdict of 'not guilty', the invading police from St Paul's could again be routed and sent packing.

Zigzagging across England, without orators or radical tacticians within their ranks, a front line of young resistance was propelled by urgent reactive necessity to act in the same way. In the north of England, in Bradford in 1981, twelve young Asians put together Molotov cocktails — rags stuffed into milk bottles filled with petrol — to be armed in case the broadcast warning was true that fascists were on their way to attack the Bradford Asian community. Charged with having made bombs, each young defendant was reinforced in his courage to articulate the same fundamental concept — the universal right of necessary self-defence — and to explain to the jury the experience of Asians at the hands of the National Front, their homes set alight, their elders beaten or killed and, as for protection by police, 'nothing ever said or ever done'. Tackling the unthinking racist structure of the criminal justice system, the beginning of the trial at Leeds Crown Court was delayed again and again when identical practices in the selection of jurors were exposed. No jurors had been summonsed from the court's catchment areas in which Asian citizens liable to jury service lived.

Two more trials in two successive years in East London, of the 'Newham Seven' and the 'Newham Eight' echoed the resounding Bradford 12 acquittals — of very young teenagers who physically took on fascists and, in one case, the police. The same collectivity of grass-roots support, mobilisation and wisdom was there to embolden them — to describe the history of attacks of Asian children even within school playgrounds, and why it was that Asian teenagers who had defended them were instead finding themselves in the dock at the Old Bailey. In a by-now-familiar precursor to their trial, the Snaresbrook court's pool of jurors had been identically exposed as having excluded areas for selection in which Asian citizens on the electoral register could be found. All these defendants could be justly found 'not guilty' if their rights could be established and the state could be taken on fairly, squarely and forthrightly.

Each of these confrontations played its part, to a degree, in checking manifestations of the state's multifaceted racism, or in so confident and overt a form — and fascist attackers paused, for a while at least, in their confident physical and on occasion fatal aggression.

But even the most triumphant of victories should never be assumed to be permanent; the courageous actions and political intelligence that created victories nevertheless required open-ended vigilance as well. Within a year of the Bristol victory, the most senior judge in England, Lord Denning, was to comment in his memoirs that the defendants in Bristol acquitted of riot, had been acquitted because they had 'Packed the jury with their own' and came from 'Countries where the truth was not known'. A week after the book's publication, two of those jurors had achieved Lord Denning's resignation and the recall and destruction of all copies of his book. But today, the right to challenge a jury in England has been abolished.

And a decade after the trial of the Mangrove Nine, the still seething resentment in the Notting Hill police canteen, 'Mangrove 1, Notting Hill Police 0', fuelled a fresh Mangrove raid, no longer targeting vocal activists but adopting an easier recourse — the planting of soft drugs on a few old-timers. And when that trial had increased the score to 'Mangrove 2, Notting Hill Police 0', and a further decade later an even bolder planting of hard drugs resulted in a score of '3-0', each successive trial had demanded the retelling of history to explain the motivation — revenge — by a police force expected to have learned from the bitter lessons of the past.

Repeated trials nevertheless took their toll — the Mangrove, albeit vindicated, struggling simply, peacefully, to serve food in a safe and tranquil environment, had been swamped by two decades of court hearings, trials and defence, and swamped too by the gentrification of Notting Hill, aided and abetted by its police. It is marked today by a blue plaque and the memories of the surviving foot soldiers. Yet every analysis, thesis, piece of organisation and learning that emanated from the ideas of a small organisation linked to that plaque, that found its place in the lives of ordinary people joining in their struggles and their formulation of the righteous demands that 'radicalism and reason in their proper proportion' can be seen to have been even more urgently relevant and needed by the neglected Grenfell Tower residents and the betrayed Windrush generation — for all of whom equal rights and equal power were as ruthlessly ignored and destroyed as for others decades before.

It is the children of the Bradford and Newham defendants who are today part of a different suspect community, defined no longer as 'Young Asians' but as 'Muslims'. Stopped, questioned and searched in their tens of thousands at ports of entry under open-ended Terrorism Act coercive powers, they are accused on the basis of secret evidence of facilitating increasingly ambi-tious executive control, in juryless courts. Programmes aimed at their generation, at 'de-radicalisation', targeting 'extremist' thinking and requiring pledged allegiance to 'British values', impose a statutory duty on teachers and doctors to report to the police signs of deviation. This is, of course, a moment of crisis in our history, a moment such as would have demanded the brilliant analysis and inspired reaction of the movement that embraced the Mangrove Nine and *Race Today*. The voice that was Darcus Howe's, after all, defined itself by the proud title of radicalism, daring to think as an 'extremist' and able to cut with an intellectual machete through the thickets of the different prejudices the UK now requires be formally accepted as essentially 'British'.

It is nevertheless quite wrong to think that that organisa-tion has left us without recourse. In struggling to resist the breath-taking reach of new state oppression, to remember that the England of the 1970s and '80s too was intended to be, and was, a brutal, cruel and crushing experience, demands remembering and understanding equally the concepts and strategies by which it was combated — and the energy, courage and stamina that was demanded of the combatants. It is with gratitude that we can revisit what has gone before.

Further Information

BOOKS

Michelle Alexander, *The New Jim Crow — Mass Incarceration in the Age of Colorblindness* (The New Press, New York) 2012

B.Bowling, R. Reiner and J.Sheptycki *The Politics of the Police* 5th.ed. (Oxford University Press)   2019

Robin Bunce & Paul Field, *Renegade: The Life & Times of Darcus Howe* (Bloomsbury, London) 2017

Angela Davis, *Freedom Is A Constant Struggle* (Haymarket, London) 2016

Paul Field, Robin Bunch, Leila Hassan, Maragret Peacock (eds) *Here To Stay, Here To Fight — A Race Today Anthology* (Pluto Press, London) 2019

James Forman Jr, *Locking Up Our Own - Crime & Punishment in Black America* (New York), 2017

DeRay McKesson, *On The Other Side of Freedom —The Case For Hope* (One World, London) 2019

Simon Peplow, *Race and Riots in Thatcher's Britain* (Manchester University Press) 2018

Brian Richardson (ed) *Say It Loud - Marxism & the Fight Against Racism* (Bookmarks, London) 2013

Bryan Stevenson, *Just Mercy* (Scribe Publications) 2015

Satnam Virdie, *Racism, Class and the Racialized Outsider* (Red Globe Press) 2014 edition

Alex Vitali, *The End of Policing* (Verso) 2017

Alex Wheatle, *East of Acre Lane* (Harper Collins, London) 2001

Keeanga-Yamahtta Taylor, *From #Blacklivesmatter to Black Liberation* (Haymarket, Chicago) 2016

REPORTS
Leslie Scarman, *The Brixton Disorders, 10 — 12 April 1981: The Scarman report: report of an inquiry* (Harmonsworth, Middlesex: Penguin Books) 1981

Sir William Macpherson, *The Stephen Lawrence Inquiry - Report of an inquiry by Sir William Macpherson of Cluny https://assets.publishing.service.gov.uk/government/uploads/ system/uploads/attachment_data/file/277111/4262.pd*f

ARTICLES
Chris Harman, 'The Summer of 1981: a post-riot analysis', *International Socialism*, Autumn 1981 *https://www.marxists.org/archive/harman/1981/xx/riots.html*

Linton Kwesi Johnson, 'Trust between the police and the black community is still broken', *Guardian* newspaper 28th March 2012 *https://www.theguardian.com/commentisfree/2012/mar/28/ trust-police-black-community-riots*

FILM
Injustice — dir **Ken Fero** (Migrant Media) *http://www.injus-ticefilm.co.uk/*

ORGANISATIONS

Darcus Howe Legacy Collective
darcushowe.org/

The George Padmore Institute
georgepadmoreinstitute.org

Inquest
www.inquest.org.uk/

Institute of Race Relations
irr.org.uk

The Monitoring Group
www.tmg-uk.org

Stand Up To Racism
www.standuptoracism.org.uk, @AntiRacismDay

StopWatch
stop-watch.org

United Families and Friends Campaign
uffcamapign.org